Fabrications

Fabrications

OVER 1000 WAYS TO DECORATE
YOUR HOME WITH FABRIC

KATRIN CARGILL

Photography by
JAMES MERRELL

Main Text by
JILL BLAKE

A BULFINCH PRESS BOOK
LITTLE, BROWN AND COMPANY
BOSTON • NEW YORK • TORONTO • LONDON

To my sweet mother and father

First North American Edition
First paperback printing, 1998

Library of Congress Cataloging-in-Publication Data
Cargill, Katrin.
          Fabrications: Over 1000 ways to decorate
      your home with fabric / Katrin Cargill:
      photography by James Merrell. – 1st U.S. ed.
          p.   cm.
      "A Bulfinch Press book."
      ISBN 0-8212-2590-1 (pb) ISBN 0-8212-2083-7 (hc)
      1. Textile fabrics in interior decoration. II. Merrell, James.
    III. Title.
    NK2115.5.F3C37   1994
    747'.9–dc20
                                                    93-28744

Bulfinch Press is an imprint and trademark of
Little, Brown and Company (Inc.)
Published simultaneously in Canada by
Little, Brown & Company (Canada) Limited

Printed and Bound in Hong Kong.

Contents

Int

roduction

The starting point for creating a stylish interior is to consider the practicalities of the basic structure of the space, the lighting and plumbing arrangements, the items of furniture in question and the various surfaces of the room. With these as a basic framework there are numerous allies which you can summon to your aid – in particular color, pattern and texture. Each of these elements will help you to create mood and ambience by setting a certain style and providing textural contrast and variety of form. These may also be implemented to improve the proportions of a room, to enhance attractive architectural features or, alternatively, to disguize unsightly ones. Throughout this book you will find exciting ideas to use a host of soft furnishings, textiles and trimmings, from the simple to the sophisticated, for every part of the home.

When you consider the almost limitless possibilities for color schemes, furnishing and room styling – the enormous color palette, the endless lengths of exciting fabric, the thousands of paints and different wallcoverings, carpets and floorings – the first question must be what to choose?

Most schemes start with color because the hues that you choose for the main surfaces, floors, ceilings and walls, window treatments, soft furnishings, accents and accessories will give your room a particular ambience. You can use color to heat up cold rooms or cool down hot ones, to create a warm, intimate feeling in a large, stark area, or give an impression of space and elegance to a small room, or to reproduce a specific period feel. It will help to bring an impression of sunshine into a dark basement or a fresh, country atmosphere into a gray urban interior. Use color to create a stimulating or a calming environment, to emphasize an interesting feature or to camouflage an unsightly one.

Colors come in two basic categories. Cool or receding tones include blue, blue-green, green, blue-lilac and some grays. These seem to retreat and have the effect of creating a calm atmosphere and making a space appear larger, especially if you use pale tones on the main surfaces. However, cool colors can give a room a chilly feel, so they are best used in warm rooms or where fairly intensive activity takes place. In contrast, warm or advancing colors appear to come toward you. This category – which includes red, pink, orange, apricot, peach, yellow, terra-cotta and tan – will make an area more enclosed, cozy and inviting, but this can be claustrophobic in a limited space so aim to use the paler values in small rooms, or on more modest surfaces. A value describes the lightness or darkness of a color, or the tint, tone or shade of a hue.

There are also the neutrals. The only true neutrals are black, white and gray. However, there are also some "accepted" neutrals, which include beige, cream, mushroom, off-white and the natural colors of materials such as wood, cane, marble, brick, stone, raw wool, flax, linen and undyed cotton. Neutrals can be warm or cool and work as either advancing or receding colors. They often act as a link or background to a scheme, although they can also be used to create a restrained and relaxing atmosphere. If you are working with neutral shades, it is essential to add plenty of textural variety and contrast to the scheme, and it also helps to add some sharp color accents.

The way that you put colors together will result in success or failure, whether you use a harmonious or a contrasting scheme. Monochromatic schemes – when only one basic color is used, but with changes in value and intensity – are harmonious. These are sometimes called blend-and-tone or tone-on-tone schemes; they can be cool or

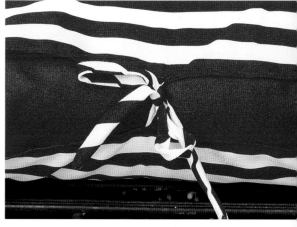

Above Rich, striped satin is used to upholster an ornate *chaise longue* and bolster. The stripe is used on the cross for decorative trimming.

Below A shaped valance or pelmet is edged in contrasting fabric and decorated with a starfish. The cotton drape is caught to one side of the window by a wooden boss fronted with a starfish.

Opposite Primary colors set against white make a strong statement. Here, fringed red and white antique linen napkins on blue and white china make a crisp impact.

Left In a high-ceilinged hallway below a wall hung with old parchment documents, a duo of chairs with the seats upholstered in bold stripes of red, white and blue silk draw the eye.

Above Contrasting striped cotton piqué fastened with ties spices up a plain pillow or cushion. The outer cover can easily be removed for laundering.

warm, depending on the basic color. A cool, fairly pale monochromatic scheme will help to create an illusion of space and light. It is essential to choose enough contrast within the tones if the result is to work well. Choose the deepest value for floors and furniture, a mid-tone for the walls and a lighter one for the ceiling. As rooms decorated monochromatically need to be contrasted with a neutral shade – and benefit from a few contrasting accents and accessories – combine all the tones in the drape fabric, plus a touch of neutral and an accent. Contrasting or complementary schemes are created by using colors which are opposite each other on a color wheel. These are sometimes called opposite hues. The "mix" is far more exciting than a harmonious one and can be highly stimulating, especially if fairly strong tones are used, so the atmosphere will not be very relaxing. It is better to use different tints and tones of the colors to create a successful complementary scheme.

One "secret" of professional decorating is the addition of contrasting accent colors to a scheme. If you opt for a mainly pale, cool scheme, add rich, bright and hot colors; if you decide on predominantly rich, warm shades, then introduce some sharp, cool contrasts. In the same way you can liven up a neutral scheme with a strong color. Add these accents in your accessories, perhaps as trimmings on drapes or curtains, in pillow or cushion covers, to pipe or trim upholstery, as tablecloths and napkins or for towels and linens. These in turn can reflect the colors of surrounding flower arrangements, collections of china and glass or pictures and prints. Good decorating and soft furnishing schemes do not rely on color alone – patterns and textures play an

essential part too, and these elements must be selected just as carefully as color and blended together with equal skill. They will help to style the room and give it the right look, from modern minimalist to something with a more distinct period feel. Both add an extra dimension to a scheme which color alone cannot provide.

Bold patterns are akin to warm colors as they appear to come toward you and so will be dominant; they will also make a large area seem less intimidating and more cozy and intimate. If you use them in a small space the effect can be overpowering and walls, ceiling, windows and floor will all appear to close in. Strong patterns also create a busy and stimulating atmosphere, which may be suitable for halls, family rooms, children's rooms and well-used bathrooms, but less desirable on the main surfaces in rooms where you want to relax. Small-scale patterns are akin to cool colors as they appear to recede. They can seem somewhat bland unless the color scheme is an interesting one, and used over a large area they tend to fade into insignificance. Small designs and patterns will help to create an impression of space in a small area. Imagining finished results can be difficult, so before you reach a decision try to see as large a sample as possible – if necessary borrow show-lengths of fabric on approval, or buy a complete roll of wallcovering so that you can try before you buy. Look at samples on the correct plane. Examine a possible wallcovering horizontally, next to, and opposite the window; hold window dressing fabric against the light and gathered vertically as it will be when made up into drapes or curtains, or pleated horizontally if it is to be tailored into shades or blinds.

If you find choosing a decorating scheme difficult, you can make a start with a patterned, multicolored piece of upholstery, drape or curtain fabric, carpet, wallcovering or border, then echo the

Above opposite The printed linen cover on this wing chair shows perfect pattern alignment.

Below opposite A remnant of black and white *toile de Jouy* is made into a coolie lampshade.

Above A rich antique *toile de Jouy* hangs happily alongside a modern interpretation and is lined with a strong woven check.

various colors on the other surfaces in the room. Begin with the main pattern and work up the scheme from there – note that a design looks more "fluid" and interesting when made up into softly draped window treatments, and drapes or curtains can seem quite different when drawn back to each side of the window from when they are pulled across it.

Color matching must be done carefully. Take a sample of your chosen fabric with you when you shop for the rest of the scheme. If this is not possible, color match to a paint manufacturers' color chart or use pieces of colored paper, wool or embroidery silks as reference. Note also the most dominant colors and once armed with these color examples, shop around for the rest of your scheme. Obtain samples which are as large as possible and bring them home with you. If you are only offered an insignificant snippet, take a note of the name of the collection, the name or number of the design, the number or letter of the colorway and contact the manufacturer for a larger piece. If this is not possible, it is often worth buying a small length of the fabric or a roll of the wallcovering or a border. Look at these samples all together in the room where you propose to use them and under exact lighting conditions – this means under both day and night lighting.

Texture works in a similar way to color and pattern and will help you to create atmosphere and style. There are different types of texture, so try and achieve a balance between them just as carefully as when choosing a pattern and plain "mix" and when selecting harmonious or contrasting color schemes. Shiny textures, which include metals, glass, ceramic tiles, marble, gloss and vinyl silk paint, laminates, glazed and silky fabrics and light-reflecting wallcoverings, all bounce back light and consequently they make the color of the surface look brighter. They can also create a "busy" and sometimes chilly feel. So shiny textures work in the same way as advancing colors and bold and dominant patterns, but they can serve to make a space seem larger because they reflect light. A room with too many shiny surfaces can be quite uncomfortable to live in, but some glossy textures are essential for stimulation and contrast.

Rough textures, such as carpet, sisal, coir and rush matting, brick and stone, cork, rough-hewn wood, riven slate, coarsely woven fabrics, hessians, linens, tweeds, soft velvets and wool, matte and rough-cast paints, will all absorb light. They appear to "swallow" the color, so reducing the impact and making the surface seem duller, more subtle, or in some cases richer. These textures create a calm and more relaxed atmosphere, and can actually absorb sound. So they work like the receding colors and quiet patterns. A room with plenty of soft and rough textures can be very comfortable and cozy, but may also be stifling; again good textural contrast is needed to offset them.

Light-filtering textures, for example, lace, nets, fine muslin or calico, voiles, open-weave sheers, slatted and rattan shades or blinds, cane, basketwork, pierced and fretwork screening and trellis all allow the light to pass through them, at the same time diffusing it. This gives the texture a fragile, delicate and almost ethereal quality, and will make the color appear paler and more subtle. These textures work in the same way as the neutral shades and can provide a much-needed link between contrasting colors, "quarrelling" patterns and rough, soft and shiny textures. They will often add that essential contrast needed to complete a successful scheme.

Opposite From the finest sheer to the heaviest natural fiber, texture dictates the visual as well as the tactile qualities of cloth. The apparent color of fabric is also affected by its texture; the color value changes according to the light that the fabric is viewed under. Here, a rough burlap or hessian with self-piping drapes into gentle folds because of its heavy texture.

Left Fine cotton drapes shown in detail. The fabric falls into natural soft folds behind a boss decorated with a starfish. A beach theme is echoed by miniature sea shells that are carefully hand-sewn along the leading edge of the drape.

Below More delicate still is a fine cotton voile loose cover tied to a wicker chair. Light filters through the gauze-like fabric.

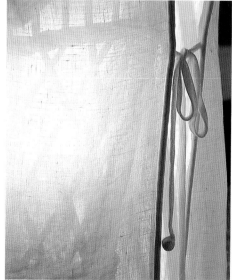

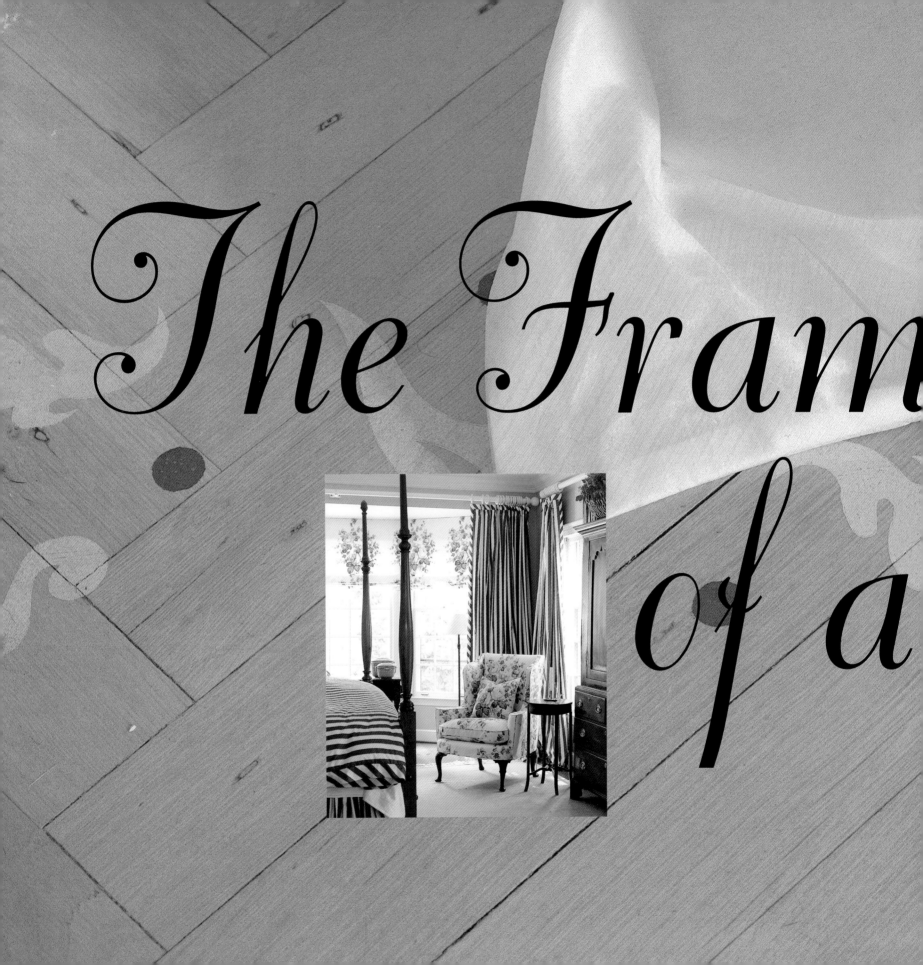

The Fram

of a

ework
Room

Before making any decisions, professional interior designers start work by looking at the framework of the room, just as a dress designer looks at the build and coloring of a client. Like people, rooms vary in size and proportion, and in the real world most are short of the designer's ideal. Dress designers start by taking their client's measurements to transfer to a dummy; the interior designer's equivalent is to draw up a floor plan. In both cases, the job of the designer is to make the best of the good features and distract from the poor ones. As well as looking at the bones being decorated, designers will always take into account the lifestyle of their clients. Ideally, fabric choice should be a happy marriage of taste and practicality. Being able to care for the fabric and keep it in good condition is important; the first prerequisite for any cloth is that it drapes well and looks and feels glorious. Textiles have a wonderful ability to carry sensual qualities into a room and make it special.

ℰARLY WINDOWS consisted of simple arrow slits used for defensive purposes, to let out smoke and fumes and let in a small amount of light. Later, a rough wooden shutter may have provided some protection from the elements and animal skins or oiled cloth were used to insulate dwellings before the introduction of glazed windows in the mid 16th century. Originally, textiles were used as decorative hangings to cover rough wall surfaces and protect against damp, cold and drafts; they were also draped over beds for privacy and warmth. Most of these hangings were portable, so they could be carried on "progresses", or journeys, from castle to castle, or taken down during the summer. Legend has it that the first "curtain" was invented when a medieval traveller, arriving at an inn on a cold winter's night, stuck his sword into the lintel above the window and draped his cloak over it! Certainly early drapes or curtains were utilitarian and consisted of a piece of fabric which was simply fixed at the top of the window and fell well short of the floor. Pairs of drapes or curtains which pulled to each side of the window were first seen in Europe at the end of the 16th century.

From this time on, fabrics and furnishings became fashionable and increasingly luxurious accessories. By the 19th century windows were lavishly draped, often in an architectural style which echoed the overall design of the interior. To prevent drafts and guard against the sun fading carpets and upholstery, windows were often over-dressed and swathed in layers of fabric. Toward the end of the 19th century, with the Arts and Crafts movement, there was a shift toward simpler interior decoration and a growing interest in Oriental and particularly Japanese design. As a result, window treatments became plainer and consisted of roller shades or blinds, combined with drapes or curtains which were gathered up and suspended from a pole.

At the beginning of the 20th century, Art Nouveau and Art Deco influences were evident but were followed by a move toward minimalist decorating based on the adage that "less is more". Drapes or curtains were often simple sheers and streamlined aluminum Venetian shades or blinds screened windows in both domestic and commercial situations. More recently, there has been a trend toward using more opulent treatments. However, one of the advantages of decorating with fabric today is that the possibilities are endless.

Window treatments

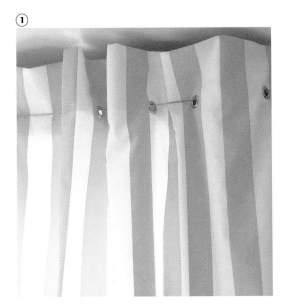

①

③

②

④

① A detail of the heading of the window treatment that is shown on page 15. The loosely gathered striped fabric hangs from a stainless steel wire that has been threaded through a series of metal eyelets punched into the cloth. In this way, the drape can glide to open and close easily along the wire.

② Knotted ties attach a double-layered drape to wooden rings strung along a pole. Cotton muslin in white and pale blue has been sewn together to create an ethereal, light-diffusing effect.

③ A double set of unlined drapes frame a French window and are attached to a brass rod with a series of tied bows. The outer drapes are held back by a pair of brass tie-backs decorated with painted porcelain.

④ Poles or rods can be covered in a narrow tube of fabric – in this case dupion silk. The fabric-encased pole just slips through the pocket-headed drapes.

You can choose almost any style, from the most spartan treatment to something that is highly sophisticated. There have never been better aids available for making and hanging window dressings and the choice of fabrics has never been wider. When it comes to choosing a window dressing there are many aspects to consider. First, look at the basic shape and size of the window as objectively as possible. If it is a beautiful architectural feature in its own right, or if there is a magnificent view, don't swathe it in fabric. Instead, choose a simple treatment which will enable the shape or vista to be enjoyed to the full. Sometimes such windows need not be covered at all – for instance, if they are not overlooked and if insulation from the cold or strong sunlight is not required. If the reverse is the problem, and the window is unsightly or the outlook dismal, or if the room lacks interest and light, then screen the window with an unusual or brightly colored treatment which will liven up the interior and help to obscure the view.

Second, look at the number and style of windows in your room. Several windows of different shapes within one room, or along one wall, will be difficult to deal with, and it usually helps to unify them with a fabric treatment. This can be done with simple drapes or curtains, suspended from a pole running right across the top of all the windows; the curtains close all the way across the wall at night and pull clear of the windows during the daytime, stacking back into the corners of the room. An alternative treatment is to use a softly shirred valance or a formal cornice or pelmet on one window, combined with simple shades or blinds or shutters on the other.

Third, the style of the room itself may influence your choice of treatment. If you aim to create a simple scheme, minimalist window

treatments may be the best choice. This could be basic shades or blinds or a lambrequin echoing the shape of the frame combined with unfussy drapes or curtains, with a slotted or tied heading on a pole.

If the room has a particular period flavor, or if you want to impose one on a somewhat featureless building, research the authentic look carefully. In order to imitate the styling correctly, study books and paintings of the era and visit museums or stately homes.

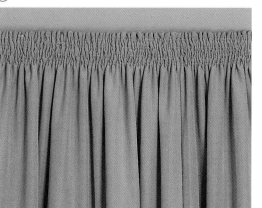

(5) In a sunny kitchen window an antique cotton tablecloth is simply clipped over a wooden pole. The fold along the top creates an attractive valance.

(6) For full drapes or curtains generous gathering is required. Here, finely woven wool is tightly smocked to give a neat heading.

(7) Light cotton tightly gathered on heading tape is tied to rings along a pole to form a pretty drape. The fabric is given a decorative finishing touch with three horizontal rows of corded piping sewn into the fabric. The bedroom chair is upholstered in *toile de Jouy*.

NAPKIN DRAPES

Materials

Basic sewing kit (see page 176)
Enough fringed napkins to make up a pair of
drapes and a gathered pelmet or valance
Lining fabric
Backing fabric
3 in/7.5 cm drape or curtain tape

The same method applies to making both drapes or curtains and the gathered valance or pelmet. For measuring up a window, see Techniques, page 182.

1 Lay the backing fabric right side up on a flat surface. Position the napkins in a patchwork pattern, right side up, leaving a hem allowance around the four sides of the backing fabric – 2½ in/6.5 cm at the top, 1½ in/4 cm at either side and 5 in/13 cm at the bottom. Pin and baste the napkins in place.

2 Turn the whole panel over so that it is wrong side up. Fold in the 1½ in/4 cm allowance down each side and pin and baste down. Fold in the 5 in/13 cm allowance along the bottom to form a double hem and hem by hand, see Techniques page 178. Fold in the 2½ in/6.5 cm allowance along the top and press. Open out the fold and set aside the whole.

3 Cut out the lining fabric to the finished size of the drape or curtain and machine a 1 in/2.5 cm hem down each side. Machine a double 2 in/5 cm wide hem at the bottom.

Blue and white checked napkins with fringed edges are sewn in a checkerboard design to cream cotton drapes.

4 Lay the drape or curtain on a flat surface wrong side up. Place the lining square over this, right side up, leaving a ½ in/1.25 cm allowance down either side and 1 in/2.5 cm allowance at the bottom. Align both the double hems along the bottom edge. Hand sew the sides together with hemming stitch, see Techniques page 178.

5 Fold the top 2½ in/6.5 cm allowance down over the lining. Pin the drape or curtain tape along the top edge. Machine together through all the layers along the top and bottom of the tape.

6 Attach drape or curtain hooks at regular intervals along the tape. Pull the tape strings evenly as required. Repeat for the second drape or curtain and the valance or pelmet.

(1)

1. Vertical stripes in silk are headed with a border of the same fabric which runs as a horizontal stripe.

2. Strong geometric lines of striped drapes and checkerboard pillows work well together.

3. Unlined calico drapes with a smocking heading tape attached to metal rings by means of knotted ties.

4. Cast-brass rings with medallion fronts hold an antique *toile de Jouy* to a heavy wooden pole.

5. Less ornate wooden rings are an appropriate heading for a light muslin drape bordered with cotton rope.

(3)

(4)

Look at archive material available from specialist wallcovering and fabric manufacturers. Check to see how fabrics were used to drape beds, cover furniture, walls and doors. Look carefully at the window treatments and examine the means of suspension as well as the overall effect. In previous centuries "double" or even "triple" standards at the window were common, for example, lace curtains over Holland or rattan shades or blinds, under heavy braid- or fringe-trimmed drapes with ornate headings. Try to discover how many nuts and bolts were necessary in order to achieve the results.

When planning to dress windows, cover walls or ceilings, or make loose covers and accessories, always consider the practicalities of different fabrics. A darker or textured fabric will require less regular washing than a light, smooth material. In much-used areas fabrics should be easy to clean or launder so that they stay looking crisp; or they should be treated to be stain-resistant. Fabric which is required to drape well should fall in soft folds and respond to being crumpled and scrunched up. But if you want neat loose covers or tailored shades or blinds,

(5)

(6)

6 A solid metal pole can support heavy drapes.

7 8 For insulation and as a barrier to light, wool bedroom drapes are lined and interlined and bordered all around with wool limousine or pure wool cloth. The seating is upholstered in white linen.

9 A period window treated with a pair of unlined cascading silk drapes which bunch on the floor.

10 Silk drapes bordered with cut-out appliqué shapes that are stitched directly onto the main fabric.

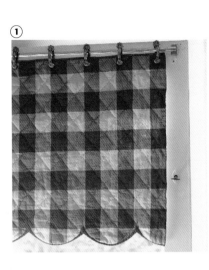

1. Antique quilted cotton with a scalloped bottom edge hangs above a door, clipped to a brass rod.

2. Dark madras cotton drapes tied to wooden rings along a pole tumble to the floor.

3. Unlined checked cotton drapes stack back against the wall to allow the French windows to open inward.

4. Thin, wrought-iron poles fit snugly into the reveal.

5. A gingham drape is swagged back in front of a split bamboo shade or blind with a long tie.

6. Calico drapes headed with looped ties slot neatly onto a wooden pole, leaving the stencilwork visible.

7. Printed cotton drapes held back with metal tie-backs to reveal window seats in an elegant living room.

8. The upper part of a kitchen door is screened by a piece of antique linen with drawn threadwork.

(6)

(8)

(7)

look for a more closely woven, less pliable fabric. Fabrics which will come into contact with heat should be insulated or checked for fire-resistance. In addition, curtains flapping above a sink or a stove in the kitchen are impractical, as are ruched shades or blinds which collect condensation and grime. Neatly tailored Roman or roller shades or blinds are a much more suitable treatment. Silk and other fabrics which are susceptible to fading and rotting are not a wise choice for sun-facing windows, even if they are lined and interlined, so select color-fast fabrics or strong-quality cloth with a tight weave for this situation unless you want to achieve a look of faded elegance.

The style of a drape or curtain is determined by several factors, apart from the actual fabric used and its color, pattern, texture and scale.

THE HEADING can actually head the top and be visible. It may have a variety of styles, for instance, it may be slotted or have individual ties, so the fabric itself provides the hanging mechanism. Or it may consist of a certain style of pleat which hides the hooks attaching the drape to the track, rod or pole. A heading may also be purely decorative, such as a stiff cornice or pelmet, a soft fabric valance or a lambrequin – all of which cover the top of the drape.

THE MEANS OF SUSPENSION may consist of a pole or rod, a track or any other means of fixing the drape or curtain above the window. With some treatments, such as poles, hooks and some discreet tracks, the means of suspension is an integral part of the overall style.

THE LENGTH OR DROP of the drape or curtain refers to how far it falls, either to the sill or to the floor. Curtains with a drop to the sill are short, neat and practical and most suitable for kitchens, bathrooms, childrens' rooms, some bedrooms, small windows and window seats.

3 For the ties: measure up six strips of patterned fabric, each should be 34 in/85 cm long and 3½ in/8.75 cm wide. Cut out.

4 Fold each strip in half, wrong side out. Machine stitch along the open edges, leaving a 1 in/2.5 cm gap in the middle of the long edge for turning right side out.

5 Using the blunt end of a pencil, turn each strip right side out and neatly hand sew the gap in the middle. Press. Repeat for all six ties and set aside.

8 Place the panel of plain fabric right side up on a flat surface. Place the panel of patterned fabric over it, right side down, aligning all four sides. Pin and baste together and machine along the top and both sides ½ in/1.25 cm in from the outside edge.

9 Turn right side out and press. The drape should now be 53 in/132.5 cm wide.

10 The red marks in the illustration above right show the position of the pleats across the top of the drape. Mark these using tailor's chalk. Measure the intervals in between the pleats accurately.

11 Pin a tie at either end of the top edge of the drape on the plain fabric side, see below. Pin four more ties in the middle of each 5 in/2.5 cm gap, as shown. The ties should fall to an even length on both sides of the drape.

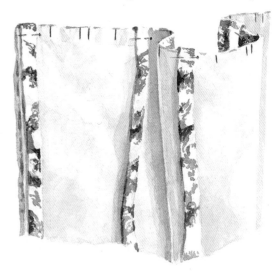

TIE DRAPES
Materials

Basic sewing kit (see page 176)
Plain fabric (see below)
Contrasting patterned lining fabric
Tailor's chalk
Wood pole (8 in/20 cm longer than
width of window)
Pair of brackets, with screws
12 wood drape or curtain rings

To make one drape or curtain, use one width of plain to one width of patterned fabric. In this example, both fabrics were 54 in/135 cm wide, to make a finished drape 53 in/132.5 cm wide. If you require a wider drape adjust your calculations for the pleats accordingly. Repeat steps 1 to 14 to make the second drape.

1 Measure up a panel of plain fabric 54 in/132.5 cm wide. Calculate the drop according to your window, see Techniques page 182. Add 5 ½ in/13.75cm to the drop. This includes a ½ in/1.25 cm seam allowance at the top and down both sides and 5 in/12.5 cm allowance for the hem. Cut out a panel of plain fabric.

2 Measure up a panel of contrasting patterned fabric to the same dimensions as the panel in step 1. Cut out.

6 For the drape: place the panel of plain fabric wrong side up. Fold up a double 2½ in/6.25 cm hem along the bottom edge. Pin, baste and hem by hand. Press.

7 Repeat step 6 with the panel of patterned fabric.

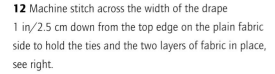

A= 2¾ in/7 cm
B = 2½ in/6.5 cm
C = ½ in/1.25 cm
D= 5 in/12.75 cm

12 Machine stitch across the width of the drape 1 in/2.5 cm down from the top edge on the plain fabric side to hold the ties and the two layers of fabric in place, see right.

Cream cotton drapes fastened with a series of ties are lined with a classical black and white *toile de Jouy* print.

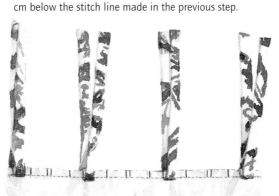

13 Move all six ties off the drape, see below, and machine stitch across the width of the drape 5 in/12.5 cm below the stitch line made in the previous step.

14 To sew the pleats: fold the first 2½ in/6.25 cm mark in half to form a pleat. Pin and machine stitch the pleat in a vertical line measuring 5 in/12.5cm in between the two parallel stitch lines. Machine through both layers of fabric. Leave a ½ in/1.25 cm gap and fold the second 2½ in/6.25 cm mark in half to form a second pleat. Pin and machine stitch as before. Leave a 5 in/12.5 cm gap where the tie is sewn and then make two more pleats until there are five sets of double pleats across the top of the drape. Press all the pleats.

15 Repeat steps 1 to 14 to make the second drape. Screw the brackets to the wall above the window frame. Slip twelve rings onto the pole and hang the pole on the brackets. Tie one pair of ties to each ring and lay the free ends of the ties down the front of the drapes.

Full-length drapes that touch the floor are more elegant and classic; these are suitable for main rooms and on long and large windows. Some drapes cascade onto the floor, creating an opulent and expensive look. However, over-long drapes are impractical in well-used family rooms, or where there is a pollution problem, or in a home with children or pets.

TRIMMINGS are decorative finishing touches. A trimmed drape or curtain may be frilled or have a turned-back leading edge, braids, a bullion fringe, cords, tassels, fabric borders or wadded edges. Trimmings include *choux* and knife-pleated rosettes and bows which are often used to finish off headings and tie-backs.

TIE-BACKS are used to hold drapes away from the window so letting in more light; they are often crescent-shaped and made of fabric which matches or contrasts with the drapes. Other types of tie-back include cord, ribbon and bosses or holds in metal or wood.

LININGS AND INTERLININGS are used to improve the way that curtains drape and fall and to help keep out light, drafts and noise. An interlining will enhance the appearance of most fabrics and will also add weight and bulk to inexpensive fabrics. However, sheers are not usually lined, as this negates their purpose, which is to create a light-diffusing effect.

Drapes or curtains come in several different types – most windows can be dressed with a pair of full- or sill-length drapes, called "draw" curtains. These either meet in the middle or overlap – the latter require a special overlapping track. They are topped with one of a variety of different hand-sewn or ready-made headings, which are stitched to the curtain and pulled up to create the desired effect; hooks or rings are fixed to the heading and in turn, suspended from rings on a pole or runners on a track.

(1) **Strong colors warm a north-facing bedroom. The wood-painted cornice or pelmet with a scalloped edge visually increases the height of the window. Heavy *toile de Jouy* drapes are held back with co-ordinating tie-backs decorated with appliquéd stars. The striped bedspread in the foreground is a hard-wearing linen.**

(2) **Drapes or curtains can be enhanced with all kinds of trimmings. On this cotton valance the top has been tightly gathered onto a pole and the edge elegantly finished with a tasselled border.**

(3) **Lightweight calico with horizontal folds machine-stitched to form a pattern hangs as a valance above a stone mullion window in a country cottage.**

④⑤ Soft green-painted window seats offset sunny, yellow printed taffeta drapes that fit neatly inside the reveals. The curtains are elegantly embellished with swags and tails that are made of the same fabric. The decorative heading is bunched at each corner above the window into a "rosette" that is held in place by means of neat hand stitches.

⑥⑦ A striking combination of checks, stripes and stars makes a a bold scheme in a little bedroom. A detail of the gathered cotton valance above the window shows a strong red trim which serves to separate the checked top treatment from the vertical stripes of the drape that hangs underneath.

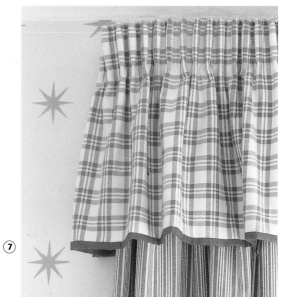

ZIGZAG CORNICE OR PELMET
Materials

Basic sewing kit (see page 176)
½ in/1.25 cm thick medium-density fiberboard
Coping saw   Medium-grade sandpaper   Marker pen
Main fabric for cornice or pelmet (see page 183)
Adhesive webbing or iron-on fabric stiffener
Ruler and set square
Contrasting fabric for edging
Straw tassels on rings
¾ in/2 cm wide touch-and-close or Velcro tape
Fabric adhesive   3 L-shaped brackets and screws

First measure the dimensions of the cornice or pelmet that you require according to the size of your window, see Techniques page 183. Using a coping saw, cut out a piece of wood board just longer than the width of the window frame and as deep as you require. Smooth the edges with sandpaper.

1 Measure the dimensions of the front of the cornice or pelmet according to your piece of wood board and the overall size that you require. Add an extra ½ in/1.25 cm turn-over allowance at the top and an extra 1 in/2.5cm allowance at each side of a panel of main fabric. Cut out. Iron the whole piece to adhesive webbing or fabric stiffener and lay flat on a hard surface.

2 Divide the width of the window by the number of zigzags that you require and make sure that both ends stop on a half or a whole zigzag. Using a set square and a ruler calculate the zigzag outline accurately on the wrong side of the panel of main fabric and mark off the zigzags with a marker pen. Cut out. Leave a 1 in/2.5 cm straight edge at either end of the panel in order to hide the ends of the wood board later (step 9). With the fabric wrong side up, turn in a double ¼ in/0.75 cm hem down each short edge and hand sew with neat stitches.

3 Cut out enough 4 in/10cm wide strips of contrasting fabric to trim each zigzag and the ½ in/1.25 cm straight ends of the bottom of the cornice or pelmet. Leave a ½ in/1.25 cm hem allowance at either end of each strip for turning under. Each strip should be 1 in/2.5 cm longer than the length of a full "V" of the zigzag outline.

4 Fold each strip in half widthways, right sides together, to form a miter that fits the angle of the "V" part of the zigzag outline.

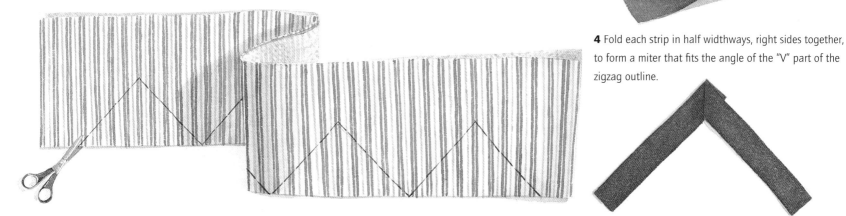

Red and white ticking drapes topped by a matching zigzag–shaped cornice or pelmet and finished with straw tassels.

5 Press the fold at one end of each strip. Open out and machine down the crease line, stopping just short of the outside edges in order to turn in the hem allowance in the next step. Snip away the excess triangle of double fabric. Repeat for each "V" of the zigzag outline.

6 Open out each V-shaped strip. Wrong side up, fold and iron in a ½ in/1.25 cm hem allowance along the inside and outside edges of the "V".

7 Lay a "V"-shaped strip right side up on the right side of the zigzag edge of the main fabric and hand sew accurately along the outside and then the inside edge of the "V". Overlap the next "V" to form the zigzag edge and turn in the short end to form a neat, vertical join. Hand sew in place and continue until the zigzag contrast edging is complete. Make two small pieces of

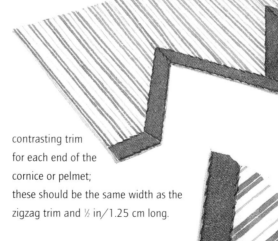

contrasting trim for each end of the cornice or pelmet; these should be the same width as the zigzag trim and ½ in/1.25 cm long.

8 Attach a drape ring to the tip of each zigzag with neat hand stitches and tie a ready-made tassel to the ring.

9 With the main cornice or pelmet fabric wrong side up, turn the top straight edge in ½ in/1.25 cm and press.

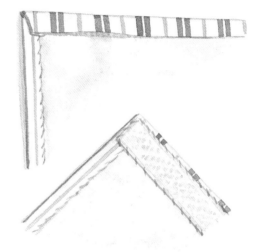

10 Cut out two strips of touch-and-close or Velcro tape to the exact length of the wood board, adding an extra ½ in/1.25 cm for each end. Hand sew one strip of tape ¼ in/0.75 cm down from the top of the wrong side of the main cornice or pelmet fabric.

11 Glue the second strip of tape along the top of the front face and two ends of the wood board and join the strips of tape together.

12 Screw three L-shaped brackets to the back of the cornice or pelmet and attach with screws to the wall above the window frame.

③

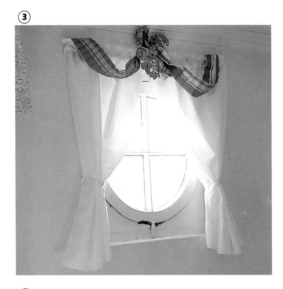

④

①

②

drape or curtain so that they can be raised on a slant. As the "pull back" point is usually quite high up the window, they restrict light less than curtains that are held open by tie-backs. In order to create the appropriate elegant effect it is essential to use a lightweight, fluid fabric such as silk, moiré or velvet.

CAFÉ CURTAINS are short, tiered curtains which are usually kept closed across the lower part of the window to screen it. Originally one tier was fixed across a café or restaurant window, just above eye level when sitting, so that the diners could not be seen from the pavement. Nowadays they are used in many different situations, but mainly for privacy and to let light in. Many types of fabric can be used – if it is sheer then the curtains can be quite full, if a thicker fabric is used this may hardly need to be gathered. Two fabrics can also be used with one lining the other – this works well with a cut-out heading which slots onto the pole.

POLE CURTAINS hang from a pole made either of wood or metal; the size and weight of the pole will vary according to the weight of the fabric that is suspended below. The drapes or curtains are attached to rings, ties, loops or pockets which thread onto the pole. The pole is supported by brackets screwed into the wall, or sometimes ceiling, and may have decorative finials at each end.

Most drapes or curtains can be closed by hand, but this may not always be practical. Pale or fine fabrics become marked or grubby very quickly and continually opening and closing curtains can weaken the fixing of a track or pole and eventually the whole construction may fall down. The alternative is to close them by means of pull rods fixed to the rings or runners, or draw them by means of a pull cord incorporated into the track or pole mechanism.

A SINGLE DRAPE OR CURTAIN can have a fixed heading above the window and can be held with a tie-back during the daytime and untied to cover the glass at night. It may be on rings and a pole, or on a track with hooks and runners to pull clear of the window.

REEF CURTAINS OR ITALIAN STRINGING is the term given to pairs of drapes or curtains that are permanently joined together at the heading. They are drawn apart by cords which are threaded through a system at the back of the

(5)

(1) Fresh muslin is swagged at the top of the window and a chair is draped with an antique linen sheet.

(2) An unlined valance with a zigzag edge conceals the track which supports a pair of white silk drapes.

(3) Fine linen drapes gathered on a rod and decorated with swags of antique ribbon dress a circular window.

(4) Cotton drapes hang below a valance made from remnants of antique quilted *toile de Jouy*.

(5) In a hallway with an elaborate Venetian chandelier a simple Battenburg lace panel screens the window.

(6)(7) For maximum daylight to penetrate, this window is given a minimal treatment of a tailored box-pleated linen valance trimmed with a cotton check.

(6)

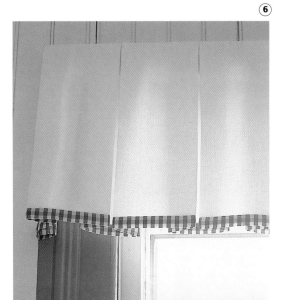

(7)

1 Measure the width of the window. Transfer this measurement onto a large sheet of paper. Fold the paper in half and draw half of the required outline of the cornice or pelmet. Cut out and open out the paper for the complete, symmetrical outline. The sides of the cornice or pelmet should extend to approximately one-third of the depth of the window. (Note that the padded and covered cornice or pelmet will add ¼ in/0.75cm width to the board.)

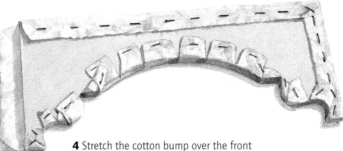

4 Stretch the cotton bump over the front of the board; make small snips to maintain the outline. Pull tight and secure with staples at the back.

5 Cut out the main fabric ½ in/1.25cm larger all around than the traced outline made in step 3.

2 Trace the paper template onto the *medium-density fiberboard. Cut out the board with a coping saw and sand down the edges.*

6 Cut out a strip of main fabric 4 in/10cm wide to measure the length of the perimeter of the pelmet board. Set this to one side.

3 With the grain vertical, place the main fabric right-side up on a flat surface and lay the board over it. If the fabric has a pattern make sure that it is square. Trace off the outline of the board with a marker pen.

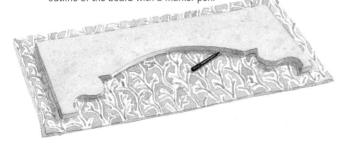

CORNICE OR PELMET
Materials

Basic sewing kit (see page 176)
Paper for template
½ in/1.5cm thick medium-density fiberboard
Coping saw   Medium-grade sandpaper
Main fabric (see page 183)
Marker pen   Staple gun
Cotton bump or padding (see page 177)
Piping cord
Plain backing fabric
Fabric adhesive   2 L-shaped brackets

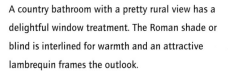

7 Make enough corded piping covered with a strip of main fabric to measure the length of the perimeter of the pelmet board, see Techniques, page 181.

A country bathroom with a pretty rural view has a delightful window treatment. The Roman shade or blind is interlined for warmth and an attractive lambrequin frames the outlook.

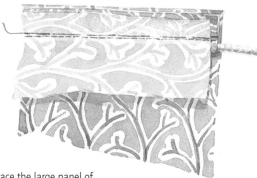

8 Place the large panel of main fabric right side up and baste together the corded piping and the 4 in/10cm strip of fabric, wrong side up, as shown. Seam the layers together, following the outline of the trace stitch line made on the panel in step 3. Turn right side out and iron.

9 Stretch the cover over the padded board and staple the excess main fabric to the back of the pelmet. Keep the fabric cover tight and make sure that the piping lies straight along the front edge.

10 To neaten the back, cut out a panel of the plain backing fabric 1 in/2.5 cm smaller than the overall back of the pelmet. Fold the edges under and stick the backing down firmly with fabric adhesive.

11 Fix two strong L-shaped brackets to the back of the pelmet with screws. Drill or nail holes to accommodate rawplugs and screws to secure the brackets just inside the window frame.

There are various ways of suspending and heading drapes or curtains which will give them a certain style. When you are looking at your windows objectively, determining the design and possibly measuring up, note the following practical points: will the frame of the window take fixings for shades or blinds or curtains? How easy is it to install a pole or a track on the wall above the window? How much headroom is there above the window to allow for fixing the heading? These points will influence the choice of type of fixing, and consequently the weight and possibly the finished length of the drapes or curtains. It is also important to make sure that window frames and plasterwork are in as good a state of repair as possible; do any restoration work before the room is decorated and the new fittings installed.

Architectural features in a room will affect planning a window treatment. Consider the amount of wall space, the position of radiators or the depth of any dado, baseboard or skirting under the window and any molding or coving above it. Take into account the position of light fixtures – sometimes wall lights are placed in between or to the side of long windows or central pendants come just in front of the window. Also, is there a fitted architrave around the window and is the window itself recessed?

Headings which are separate from the drapes and hide the track from view are usually seen as a more formal way of dressing a window. Despite their somewhat grand image, soft fabric drapes with a frilled or box-pleated valance can give an otherwise ordinary treatment an attractive extra flourish. The more rigid cornice or pelmet can be tailored into many different and interesting shapes – flowing baroque curves, castellated and scalloped effects and tassel-trimmed triangles. These can all echo

①

the style of the scheme, and the architectural character of the room. Both types of top treatment can be combined with shades or blinds instead of drapes, and in some cases they are allowed to stand alone and frame an uncurtained window.

CORNICES OR PELMETS are usually cut from plywood or hardboard, or a buckram "stiffener" into the desired shape and are then covered with fabric. They can also be painted, using any number of different techniques, papered, stenciled, decorated with borders or relief

②

① An informal country check is used to treat the windows in this high-ceilinged bedroom. The tie-backs are made of matching cotton fabric.

② Drapes or curtains can be caught back simply and effectively by banding a length of hemmed fabric around them two or three times, tying the ends in a bow and looping this over a hook on the wall.

③④ A cottage room that has been decorated in a nautical style. The bed has been suspended from the ceiling rafters by means of lengths of thick hemp rope, giving a hammock effect. The ungathered fixed drapes or curtains at the window are patterned with aqua-colored fish. The nautical theme has even been extended to the tie-backs which have been fashioned from metal sail boat cleats, used for tying ropes or lines to.

⑤ Yellow taffeta drapes are caught back by means of a multi-colored striped velvet, which is made up into a padded tie-back and then looped onto a metal hook. An unlined fabric hanging at the window allows a soft light to filter into the room.

⑥ Somewhat informal black and white cotton mattress ticking for drapes is instantly smartened by tying the fabric back with a formal antique bronze sunburst, that has been fixed to the wall.

⑦ A simple brass tie-back holds a narrow drop of cotton away from the window. Wall-mounted swing tie-backs are easy to use and lend a classical touch.

⑧ A strong-colored *toile de Jouy* tie-back is edged in contrasting red cotton and has red appliqué stars which echo the miniature stars in the wallpaper.

⑨ Two sets of unlined drapes or curtains made of contrasting fabrics are a typical Swedish window treatment. Often a floral print is used in conjunction with a country check. In this case, a tie-back in one of the fabric patterns has been looped over a metal bracket that is fixed to the wall.

⑩ On a white cotton duck tie-back lengths of machine-stitched narrow satin ribbon in a contrasting color create a decorative pattern. A plain fabric can be enhanced by the creative use of machine stitching.

③

④

⑤

⑥

⑦

⑧

⑨

⑩

①

②

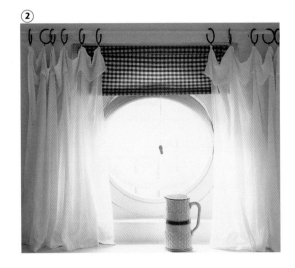

decorations made from fibrous plaster. This basic form is then mounted on a wooden cornice or pelmet board above the drape or curtain heading, which is usually above the window itself, and this incorporates the track to which the drapes or curtains themselves will be attached. A cornice or pelmet can also hide the mechanism of a roller or any other type of shade or blind, and need not always be combined with drapes or curtains.

LAMBREQUINS are rigid cornices or pelmets which follow the form of the window across the top and down the sides, giving the window a neatly tailored look. They are more usually used in conjunction with a roller or Roman shade or blind to give an attractive architectural outline. Combined with the fullness of drapes or curtains, a lambrequin can be too bulky.

VALANCES are much softer than cornices or pelmets and are made entirely from fabric, although they can be lined and interlined to give them more substance. They are really very short curtains, suspended above the main drapes or shades or blinds to hide the top. They are hung by means of a valance track – which is usually combined with the drape track, forming a

③

⑥

④

⑤

① A drop of fine linen is held back with a wooden tie-back and the heading is gathered onto a rod.

② A red and white gingham shade or blind coupled with thin muslin drapes screen a round bedroom window. White muslin allows light to filter into the interior.

③④ A bold brass rosette holds aside a plain muslin drape which is trimmed with a cotton bobble fringe.

⑤ Spotted sheer voile drapes diffuse light into a modern living room. On the floor, the circular coir matting is bound with cotton and stencilled around the edge.

⑥ Swathes of fine muslin at the windows and white linen upholstery lighten a north-facing living room.

① A trio of tall floor to ceiling windows in a 19th-century house are given maximum impact with a minimal treatment. Long panels of linen suspended from *portière* rods can be swung to control the amount of light that enters the room.

② *Portière* rods that are fixed to the frame of a window or door offer a practical solution when frequent opening and closing are required.

①

double track – or fixed onto a wooden board. In some cases the valance may be suspended from a pole with the drape, in which case the two may be sewn together at the top, or it can hang from a separate pole above the window, with the drape fixed to a frame-mounted track or pinned to the frame itself. In order to achieve perfect proportions the depth and width of cornices or pelmets and valances must be worked out carefully. As a general rule, the lowest point of a cornice or pelmet, valance or swag should be

about one-sixth of the window height, or the finished length of the drapes, if these are to touch the floor and the window falls short of it. For measuring up windows for making drapes and shades or blinds at home, see page 182. Test what the final effect will look like by hanging fabric, or old sheets, to simulate the length and fullness of the treatment. Use templates cut from paper to the proposed depth and shape and pin them to the top of the window – stand well back to judge the result.

All these treatments can be trimmed in an interesting or unusual way and can echo the leading edge on drapes, or the hem on shades or blinds and curtains. In a room where borders or decorative molding or cornices have been used, the trimming on the cornice or pelmet or valance can repeat the motif or shape of the relief decoration – in some cases this may have to be stenciled or painted. There are also some companion fabric and wallcovering borders available to help tie a scheme together.

(3) A view of a Roman shade or blind which falls in evenly spaced linen pleats and has a boxed heading.

(4) On a landing, a linen Roman shade or blind with a checked border and trim is finished with long ties.

(5) In a modern living room the windows are clad in linen Roman shades or blinds to keep the interior light.

(6) Fine white linen hangs beautifully in wide horizontal pleats on an unlined shade or blind.

(7) A detail of a cotton seersucker shade or blind which is held at the required level by a pair of long cotton ties that run from top to bottom of the main fabric panel.

The choice will depend on the formality of the treatment and the style of room decoration and also on the texture of the main fabric. Braids, bullion fringe, tassels, gimp and cords can all be used for more opulent treatments and rich fabrics such as silks, moirés, brocades and velvets. Soft bobble fringe, lace and *broderie anglaise* are ideal for trimming sheers, voiles and muslin or calico, cheesecloth and *piqué*. Deckel-edged braids, frills, ribbon bows and flat braids suit simpler window treatments and combine well with crisp chintzes, cottons, linens and closely woven twills.

Color contrasts also have to be considered when selecting trimmings. A plain, contrasting color or one which picks out one of the tones in a multicolored patterned fabric will help to define the edge or the shape of a cornice or pelmet, valance or swags and tails, or will emphasize the style of a heading. If you want the window treatment to look all of a piece, trim any top treatment with a self-color.

So many different types of drapery hardware are now available that it is sometimes confusing and difficult to make a choice, but once you have decided on a drape or curtain styling you will know the method of suspension you need. It is important to make sure that the

1 A cotton butter muslin valance or pelmet with swagged drapes held back by wooden tie-backs serve to formalize country gingham shades or blinds.

2 The addition of a pretty lace border along the bottom of a plain Holland shade or blind turns an ordinary treatment into something more decorative.

3 Heart-shaped wrought-iron finials at either end of a pole add interest to an otherwise box-shaped window that is screened by a country gingham Roman shade or blind. The perimeter is self-edged using the check on the cross.

track, pole, rod or wire is going to be strong enough to support the drapes or curtains, as some plastic tracks are not strong enough to take heavyweight fabrics, and that they are going to open and close easily, as rings and poles are sometimes jerky in operation.

If you are using fabrics which mark easily, you should choose a type of track which has a cord pull or cording set so that you can draw the drapes or curtains simply at the pull of a cord without harming the cloth. Some of these are electrically operated and some cording sets can be added to existing tracks. Most ordinary molding or cornice poles can't be combined with pull cords, but there are special poles available which incorporate cording sets. You can use draw rods which hang behind the drapes or curtains, attached to the runners. If you want track-mounted shades or blinds, make sure that they can be raised and lowered easily.

In the case of glazed doors and some windows, you will need a track or a pole which holds the drapes or curtains away from the door or frame; in some instances you can use the special *portière* rod which rises to open and falls to close the door. If you are dressing a bay or a bow window you will want a track or pole which follows the curve. There are metal or wooden poles with metal angle joints which will follow a curve. On angled bays check the degree of the angle, as some poles can be mitered in order to accommodate this.

Cornices or pelmets require special cornice or pelmet boards which are combined with a suitable track which is mounted on the back or "ceiling" of the board. These tracks are usually made of strong metal and have an overlap in the middle. Fabric valances need a double track to support the drapes or curtains and valance separately. Most hardware manufacturers produce helpful literature. And well-stocked department stores, do-it-yourself outlets and specialist shops stock a wide selection, so it is worth looking around and comparing types.

TRACKS are made from flexible plastic and are designed to be fairly unobtrusive. They are available in various weights, including some that are designed for use with very light fabrics such as sheers and nets. Some plastic tracks have grooves with runners along the back, into which the drape or curtain hooks are slotted, others have runners which hook over the track and some types have runners and hooks combined, which slip into the heading tape. Most of these tracks are designed to be hidden when the drapes or curtains are closed.

Metal tracks are usually made from aluminum or brass and are stronger than plastic ones. They can be curved or angled to go around bays; in some cases they overlap in the middle so that there is no visible gap in the drapes or curtains when closed.

POLES are usually made from wood which may be natural, stained, painted or primed for painting yourself; others are made of metal such as brass or wrought iron; most brass poles are lacquered to prevent tarnishing. Painted metal and plastic poles are also available.

④

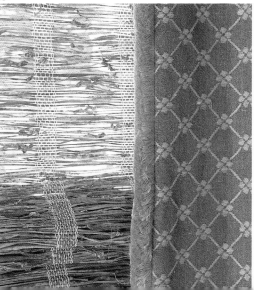

⑤

④ The leading edge of a curtain or drape has been richly trimmed with a deep cotton fringe to distinguish the fabric from the fine straw shade or blind that screens the window pane. The two different textures work well together and the straw protects the curtain fabric from the risk of fading.

⑤ To enhance the proportions of a tall, elegant window a neatly tailored Roman shade or blind has been trimmed with an inset contrasting band of fabric. The treatment serves to accentuate the strong vertical lines, so raising the apparent height of the room.

1 Measure the arch of the window. Transfer these dimensions to paper and trace onto the board. Cut the board to the required outline with a coping saw and smooth the edges with medium-grade sandpaper.

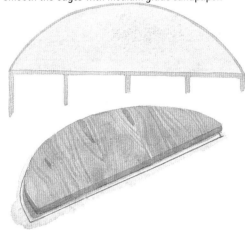

2 With the grain vertical, cut out a panel of main fabric measuring the overall drop of the window from the top of the arch to the sill (add a 9½ in/24 cm allowance for the board and hem) by the overall width of the window inside the frame.

(Add a 7½ in/19 cm side turning allowance.) Lay flat, wrong side up and fold in 3¾ in/9.5 cm down both sides and iron flat. Fold in 7½ in/19 cm along the bottom edge and iron into a crease, then open out. This crease will serve as a guide for the bottom of the finished shade or blind.

3 Cut out a piece of lining fabric the drop of the window from the top of the arch to the sill (add a 9½ in/24 cm hem allowance) by the width of the window inside the frame (add a 6¼ in/16 cm side turning allowance). Place the lining wrong side up and iron a fold 3 in/8 cm down each side. Turn over the lining fabric and lay flat.

4 To calculate where to make the pleats in the lining for the dowel or rod pockets, divide the drop of the window, from the bottom of the arch to the sill, by the number of pleats required, always ending on a half pleat. Mark with pins on both sides.

CURVED-TOP ROMAN SHADE OR BLIND

Materials

Basic sewing kit (see page 176)
Paper for template
½ inch/1.5 cm medium-density fiberboard
Coping saw   Medium-grade sandpaper
Marker pen   Main fabric (see page 183)
Lining fabric (see page 183)
Five ¼ in/0.75 cm wooden dowels or rods
15 shade or blind rings   Staple gun
Shade or blind cord and acorn pull
4 cup hooks   3 L-shaped brackets
Wall cleat with screws

5 To make the dowel or rod pockets measure a half pleat up from the bottom of the right side of the lining fabric, and make a fold large enough to accommodate the dowel or rod. Iron the fold flat and pin down. Seam along the bottom of the fold to form a narrow pocket across the width of the lining. Repeat for each pleat marked in step 4. Make each fold in the same direction.

Windows with an arched top often present a problem when it comes to choosing a window treatment. Here, a pleated Roman shade or blind follows the curve of the arch. The large red and white cotton check is also used for the loose covers on the chairs in this country kitchen.

6 Place the main fabric wrong side up on a flat surface, with the ironed folds around the perimeter facing upward. Fold the bottom 7½ in/19 cm crease in half to a double thickness and iron the fold inward.

7 Place the lining fabric square over the main fabric, with the dowel or rod pockets facing upward. The panel of lining fabric should be about ¾ in/2 cm smaller all around than the main fabric panel underneath. Align the bottom pocket with the top of the double crease at the bottom of the main fabric. Pin the two panels together around all four sides.

8 Machine stitch the main fabric and the lining together along the bottom of each pocket stitch line to hold the two layers together. Neatly hand hem the bottom edge of the shade or blind, see Techniques page 178.

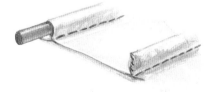

9 Insert a wooden dowel into each pocket and sew up the ends by hand.

10 Hand sew three shade or blind rings at regular intervals along each rod pocket. The rings should line up vertically. Loop the cord straight through each vertical row of rings from the bottom upward and tie with a knot to each of the three bottom rings. Leave enough surplus cord at the top to allow for pulling the whole up and down.

11 Still working on the reverse side of the shade or blind, lay the wooden board over the fabric allowance at the top and staple down, stretching the fabric over the curve so that it lies flat. Fix four cup hooks to the bottom narrow edge of the board and draw through the lengths of shade or blind cord.

12 Fix three L-shaped brackets along the top of the curve at the back of the board to attach the whole shade or blind just inside the window frame. Pull the cords together into a wooden acorn. Pull the shade or blind down to its maximum length with the pleats aligned and knot off the cords. Attach a cleat to the wall to support the cords when the shade or blind is raised.

The drapes or curtains are suspended from rings which slip over the pole and these have eyelets in them into which the hooks are slotted. They have decorative finials or end-stops which fit onto the end of the pole once the rings are in position and prevent the drapes or curtains from slipping off at either end. Poles are supported on brackets fixed to the wall, which hold the fabric well clear of the window frame. A long run of pole will need supporting in several places along the length otherwise it will bend in the middle and look unsightly. Wooden poles can be mitered to fit angled bays or combined with metal to fit around a curve. There are special metal poles which have a concealed track at the back behind a curved front and these can be fitted with an overlap and cording set.

RODS are used for nets, sheers and café curtains. These are usually made from metal which may be painted, plastic-coated or, most attractively, made in brass. The drape or curtain can be fixed to the rods by means of rings, by a scalloped top in the fabric, by decorative ties, or by a casing in the top of the drape or curtain – this can be placed part of the way down so that a frilled heading stands up above the rod. These rods are either held in place by brackets or else they can be screwed into an end-stop fixed to the window frame. There are also expandable types with a spring mechanism, which fit inside the window reveal.

WIRES are made from expandable metal which acts like a coiled spring; these are covered with plastic. The wires are fixed in position by means of screw eyes that are fixed at either end of the wire and by hooks which are attached to the frame. The hooks are slotted through a hem or a casing in the drape or curtain and can only be used with lightweight fabrics, usually nets and sheers.

① A bedroom window is half obscured by an Austrian shade or blind in printed linen. The fabric is tea-dyed in order to give it a look of faded elegance.

② Strong black and white cotton print lines the wall in a study (to do this, see the project on page 55). The co-ordinating shade or blind gives a unified scheme.

③ Pale violet quilted matelasse is given a gathered frilled edge to dress a window in a guest room.

④ Deep yellow *toile de Jouy* makes a strong impact, especially when set against bare floorboards.

*E*ARLY FORMS of wall and floor decoration consisted of tapestries, hangings and simple coverings woven from wool, linen and other natural fibers. These were overlaid on the rough walls and floors of castles and great houses, providing warmth and insulation as well as adding design interest.

In the 17th century, embossed and gilded leather was used to decorate walls; the colors were rich and jewel-like and the overall effect was one of elegance. The tanning, colors and decorating techniques were brought by the Arabs from Morocco to Spain, France and Italy and were eventually introduced to northern Europe. Other rich fabrics such as damasks, silks and brocades were all used to drape walls, and often walls and windows were treated as one area and hung with the same fabrics. Beds in bed chambers were curtained to match. Later, chintzes were imported from the East, in particular China, and used as wall hangings, while the famous *toile de Jouy* printed fabric was used for all-over treatments on ceilings, walls and windows. *Trompe l'œil* began to appear and surfaces were decorated with paint to simulate costly treatments. Marble was highly popular and decorative plasterwork, niches and statuary were also painted on walls and ceilings to look three-dimensional. In some cases, such "eye-deceivers" were painted on canvas – this was stretched on battens that were fixed to the wall and so could be removed and used elsewhere. When early wallpaper was produced it imitated the kinds of fabrics and leather that had previously covered walls. Later textiles were simulated in moiré effects and then flock appeared, giving walls a velvety texture. Flock was made by printing or stencilling a design in slow-drying adhesive onto printed canvas or thick paper and then brushing or blowing minute fibers of wool, linen, cotton or silk onto this backing. Nowadays vinyl and other synthetic wallcoverings and some textured papers echo this sumptuous velvety look and combine it with easy-care, washable qualities.

The walls are a prominent part of any interior and are seen in relation to all the other surfaces in the room. They are frequently broken up by doors, fireplaces and alcoves and in some rooms a whole wall may be almost entirely glazed, or have several windows set into it – this must be considered when you are deciding on the balance of the scheme and selecting the window treatments.

Surfaces

Opposite Saffron-yellow wool face cloth hangs from wall-mounted brass bosses and falls in soft folds to make an inviting alcove for a bed. The matching bed dust ruffle or valance has a central kick pleat and a matching wool fringe.

① In a loft or attic room at the top of a large house, the interior is given a dramatic all-over treatment with the walls and sloping ceiling covered in black and white *toile de Jouy*.

② In the same room, a detail of the edge of a fabric-covered door which is trimmed with a row of flat double piping of cotton *toile de Jouy*.

③ All sorts of fiber mattings are available as flooring. In this case, seagrass is overlaid with a white cotton rug which is fringed with jute.

Sometimes it is best to aim for unification and to use the same color, or an identical fabric or co-ordinated wallcoverings or fabrics on walls and windows. This can help to make a room appear larger and "fade" an unsightly window into the background. If you want to make the windows stand out, treat the walls to contrast with them.

The floor of a room is another main surface and needs careful consideration. Flooring can represent significant expense, so making the right choice of color, texture and pattern, or otherwise, is vital to the overall scheme. In any furnished interior some parts of the floor are bound to be obscured by pieces of furniture and perhaps rugs or other moveable coverings,

(4)

(5)

(6)

(7)

nevertheless other parts of the floor will remain visible and should complement the surrounding walls and furnishings.

Ceilings tend to be forgotten, for people rarely look up at them! However, they can be an important part of a scheme and do not always have to be painted white. If you want to make a ceiling look higher then paint it several degrees paler than the main wall color, avoiding too sharp a contrast. If you wish to lower a ceiling visually you can do it in a warm, advancing color to contrast with the walls and echo the color on the floor. Tenting a ceiling with fabric can also help to lower it physically and visually and will create an atmosphere of intimacy and warmth.

(4) A pair of lined *toile de Jouy* drapes merge with a co-ordinating fabric-covered wall. The drapes hang on *portière* rods which swing back against the wall to allow maximum light to penetrate the room.

(5)(6) The light-wood floor in a child's bedroom is embellished with a linen floor cloth edged in yellow linen scallops with neatly mitered corners.

(7) An ordinary sisal rug is smartened up with the addition of a classical tapestry border which is hand-sewn around the perimeter. You can buy inexpensive floorcloths and liven them up with trimmings.

51

There are many ways of putting fabric on walls, not forgetting that some fabrics can be paper-backed and hung as a wallpaper. Before you begin to cover a wall make sure that the surface is well-prepared. Textiles attached to a wall or a ceiling can magnify any bumps, cracks and imperfections. Ensure that the plasterwork has no lumps and bumps and treat "live" plaster which is flaking or crumbling away; any damp patches will also need to be treated.

STAPLING fabric with a strong staple gun will hold fabric on a vertical surface. The fabric can be fixed flat, which looks impressive if the pattern is bold, or pleated to give a softer, more tailored look. Dust, dirt and moisture tend to seep through walls, so it is advisable to put up sheets of wide plastic by stapling, before applying a bump lining and then an outer layer of cloth. This will retain most soiling and ensure a longer life of the wallcovering. When using fabric, always machine widths together and apply to each wall in a section. Corners and unsightly joins around doors and windows can be covered with a braid or trim.

BATTENING is an alternative method where battens are fixed horizontally across the wall, and in some cases, such as on very large walls, vertical uprights have to be included. The fabric is then stretched across the battens and tacked or stapled into place. This usually means that there will be a join where the widths of fabric meet, which will need to be seamed before putting up. Often a braid or another type of decorative trim is stuck over the join which adds visual interest to the treatment.

TRACK FIXING involves fixing special tracks around the perimeter of the wall. Using a special tool, the fabric is slipped in between the "lips" of the track and then either stretched smooth or pleated. The textile has to be seamed before

hanging so flat-fixing may create problems with joins, although these can be hidden if the fabric is pleated. Extra-wide fabrics are available and are suitable for this sort of wallcovering.

POLES, RODS OR WIRES can be fixed across the top of the wall in the same way as they are hung at windows – this is easier if there is a molding or cornice or coving instead of an angled join in between the wall and ceiling. The fabric is then made up into giant-sized drapes or curtains with the desired heading and either fixed by rings or hooks or slotted onto the rod, pole, track or wire.

①

It can be left to drape to the floor or fixed in position by tacking, stapling or repeating the heading or means of suspension parallel to the baseboard or skirting.

ROPES AND CORDS provide a means of suspending fabric on a wall less permanently. Eyelets can be stitched or punched around the edge of the fabric and threaded through with cords, ropes or ribbon – even ordinary string if it suits the fabric and the style of the hanging. These are then looped through or tied to screw

eyes fixed in the wall. This method can also be used successfully to create screens, canopies and awnings. If you prefer a more restrained look, textiles can be made into wall hangings. These are usually mounted on battens top and bottom and suspended from the wall, although poles can be used as an alternative means of suspension. For another part-wall treatment fix picture frame beading to the walls in panels and fill the space inside the frame with fabric. Also, you can buy remnants of colorful, unusually patterned fabric or beautifully textured scarves and shawls and frame them to hang as pictures on the wall. Simple frames consisting of a backing with a sheet of glass clipped around the edges are an inexpensive and simple way of displaying fabric.

Covering walls with fabric can be both exotic and practical as it helps to hide a poor surface and can also provide good insulation, especially if you use a thick fabric. As an extension to applying fabric to walls, ceilings can be tented. This is usually done using the "marquee" principle where the fabric is gathered from a central point, fanning out softly and then fixed at the edge of the ceiling or molding or cornice with pins, tacks or staples. It can also be slotted onto poles or wires fixed around the top of the wall. In high rooms a sheer textile used to create a translucent "roof" can look magical. The central point from which the textile is draped can be covered with a gathered rosette made of the same fabric. This tented technique is also used for draping beds. For a more opulent Oriental look, use ethnic fabrics such as coarsely woven Indian cotton, raw silks, kelim prints or Turkish textiles to tent the ceiling and continue down the walls to reach floor level. Pin the fabric in informal folds and catch it here and there with a cord and tassel.

(2)

(1) To contrast with a wall covered with crewelwork, panels of woven linen are hooked to the top of a window frame with eyelets.

(2)(3) Wardrobe doors ingeniously disguised in a dressing room. The upper part of each door is upholstered with tailored crewelwork while the lower part is panelled.

(4) A blue and white tablecloth is hung on a wide expanse of wall; small pleats at either end and in the middle give an attractive draped effect.

(5) Old-fashioned narrow cotton hand towels hang from metal hooks in a kitchen to form bold vertical stripes.

(3)

(4)

(5)

(6) A symphony of pattern, texture and color, this interior is a lesson in the art of mixing and matching different fabrics. The walls are covered with colorful crewelwork and the bed and upholstered screen are a riot of blue and white checked fabrics. Even the floor is covered in a patterned cotton chintz.

(7) A detail of the chintz-covered floor in the same room; the fabric was glued directly onto the floorboards and varnished to give a hard-wearing finish. It creates the illusion of a painted surface.

(6)

(7)

① A wall covered in checked linen is neatly edged with braid and the light switch is fixed over the fabric.

②③ Black and white cotton ticking covers the walls in a bedroom. The co-ordinating drapes disguise a narrow window and run across one wall; they are held back with metal bosses to frame the bed. A detail of the drapes show a neatly pleated headings.

If you want a less formal effect you can fix fabric to the ceiling in an awning style. Poles can be screwed to the ceiling and the fabric draped over them. This works well above beds, to simulate a four poster, or to define the sleeping from the sitting area in a dual-purpose room.

Fabric can be cut, draped and fixed to cover awkward wall areas and sloping ceilings, but pattern matching can be difficult so use plain or simply patterned textiles in this situation – stripes, checks and small motifs work best. If the fabric is to be fixed flat to the wall you will need to allow for accurate pattern matching and work out quantities as for wallpaper. If the fabric is to be luxuriously draped you will need to allow for matching up the pattern, where it has to be seamed, and also allow for enough fabric so that the design continues around the room. The amount you need will also depend on how full the folds are to be. Work out the quantity following the principles described for measuring up windows for drapes or curtains (see Techniques, page 182).

Types of flooring usually vary according to the particular room in the house. Highly patterned floors may complicate the task of harmonizing the scheme of a room. In contrast, plain flooring – whether an unyielding surface such as wood or stone, a rough texture like sisal or seagrass or wall-to-wall carpeting in a neutral shade – lends itself as a background to individual rugs, mats or throws.

The right choice of supplementary floor covering will help to link different elements in a furnished room and enhance the overall effect, as well as adding comfort underfoot. Rugs and matting have the advantage of being moveable. In a room where there is a predominance of plain decoration and soft furnishings a richly patterned rug or other type of temporary floor covering can provide a strong focus and may help to define a grouping of furniture. Different sorts of fabrics can be used to striking effect on the floor. For instance, ordinary mats of natural fiber such as coir or jute can be embellished with a tapestry border or a painted stencilled pattern. Flat-weave rugs, floorcloths and even panels of hard-wearing burlap or hessian or heavyweight linen can be enhanced with contrasting fabric edgings or decorative fringes or trim to make attractive temporary additions to the floor and echo parts of a scheme.

In a bedroom, the walls have been upholstered in cotton ticking and edged in double piping.

4 To make the cross band: cut out enough main fabric on the bias, see Techniques, page 181, to cover the width of the wall. The strip should be 4 in/10 cm wide. (Join strips together if necessary.)

5 Place the strip right side down and turn in a 1 in/2.5 cm fold along both long edges. Press the folds.

7 Machine stitch along the top and bottom of the strip.

8 Staple the fabric to the wall. Always start from the middle of the top of the wall and work your way outward and downward, constantly checking that the pattern is straight and square. Trim off any excess fabric once the stapling is finished. If the wall is interrupted by a window or a door, make sure that you leave sufficient allowance at the edges when cutting out in order to facilitate stapling down.

9 Make up enough corded piping to go twice around the perimeter of the wall area that is to be covered, see Techniques page 181.

10 Make double piping by laying two lengths of piping snugly against one another. Machine them together just below the cords.

11 Trim off excess fabric below the raw edges of the piping and glue the double piping, around the perimeter of the fabric walling to hide the staples. Glue the seam side of the piping down so that the rounded side faces forward.

FABRIC-COVERED WALLS

Materials

Basic sewing kit (see page 176)
Wide plastic sheeting
Padding such as polyester sheeting or interlining
Staple gun   Main fabric
Corded piping   Fabric adhesive

To calculate the amount of fabric you need, measure each wall separately. Work out how many widths of fabric you require to cover each wall and cut out enough lengths of fabric, leaving a 2 in/5 cm allowance top and bottom for stapling and a 1 in/2.5 cm allowance at either side for seaming widths together. Make sure that the wall surface is smooth, clean and dry before you begin.

1 Staple plastic sheeting over the wall and trim the edges. This will prevent dirt and dust from seeping through the fabric.

2 Cover the wall with padding, using a staple gun. Make sure that there are no gaps in the padded surface.

3 Seam together lengths of fabric measured according to the wall space you wish to cover. Press.

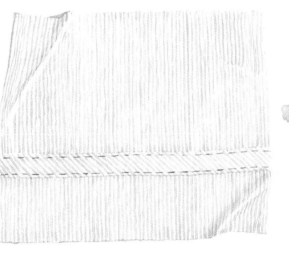

6 Place the panel of walling fabric right side up on a flat surface and baste the strip of fabric on the cross to it at the required height.

AN UNFURNISHED HOUSE is a barren structure, whatever building materials are used and the rooms in it are blank areas, composed of walls, a ceiling, a floor, one or more windows and doors and possibly a basic architectural feature such as a fireplace. In order to turn these empty spaces into a home you will need to add color, comfort and style to create mood and character and so stamp your personality onto your surroundings.

Each room – living room, dining room, kitchen, bedroom and bathroom – will also need to be designed in order to relate to the number of people who make use of it and the way that it is used. The colors, patterns and textures that you select for the various surfaces and the furnishing textiles that you use for the window treatments, upholstery and covers, flooring, drapes and cloths, accents and accessories will be the main softening influences in your home and will provide you with versatile styling "tools".

The

Rooms

A LIVING ROOM is a place to enjoy the company of family and friends or just rest and relax. Therefore it is appropriate to choose a scheme which is easy on the eye as well as hard-wearing and practical. However, this does not mean choosing a dull, dark or over-patterned scheme in an attempt to conceal dirty marks and spills.

Upholstery should be as easy-care as possible – removable loose or slip covers are often the most practical solution and have the added advantage that you can buy or make an alternative set to ring the seasonal changes. The fabric needs to be shrink- and fade-proof. Also, make sure that the zippers and any fasteners are shrink- and rust-resistant as well as color-fast and consider that buttons, frog-fastenings and simple ties offer attractive alternatives for attaching loose or slip covers and create a design feature in their own right. If you select a pattern, check or stripe ensure that the lines match neatly at the seams. Large, geometric patterns, formal dominant motifs and full-blown florals are suited to large-scale, dominant couches or sofas and chairs. Tight, tailored or fixed covers should be spongeable, or treated with an anti-stain treatment; many new pieces of upholstered furniture are sold ready-treated.

The size, shape, amount of natural daylight that the room receives, the basic architectural style and any distinguishing features should influence your choice of furnishing. And you may well want to impose a specific character on the space, or create a certain mood. Window dressings will have to be selected to suit the overall architectural style of the room and if the living room is very well-used then a washable fabric or neatly tailored shades or blinds are a sensible option. Opulent fringe-trimmed drapes or curtains which cascade to the floor are less practical in a family living area and more suited to a drawing room. In a more formal living room, less frequented by children and pets, colors can be paler, textures more luxurious or fragile, furniture less sturdy in design and window treatments more exotic.

Because the living room is usually the area used for entertaining friends you may wish to give it a sense of style. Consider its architectural character and take note of the bad points as well as the good. Look out for ceilings with decorative plasterwork, an original fireplace, sash windows with internal shutters or wood panelling. Whatever the original character of your home, try to draw attention to attractive period details.

Living rooms

Previous page
Left Dark ceiling beams and panelled and tiled walls are lightened with plenty of creamy cotton and linen.
Right Antique beds dressed with muslin canopies edged in a thick black cotton rope and linen dust ruffles or valances in a room that is beautifully schemed in black and cream.
Opposite Calico drapes hang behind a red-painted settee piled with a mix of cotton pillows or cushions.

Lighting is an important factor when selecting furnishing fabrics – always consider natural daylight when choosing colors and textures. A shiny surface, such as a silky wallcovering or fabric or a varnished surface, will reflect light and so add brightness to the room. While a light-reflecting surface helps to create an impression of space, it also emphasizes any imperfections in the surface beneath and so it is unsuitable for use on poorly plastered walls and ceilings, pitted woodwork, uneven floors and lumpy upholstery. One solution is to diffuse the strength of daylight that enters the room by means of shades or blinds or a sheer fabric at the window.

①② A couch that has been adapted from a metal-framed bed. Tufted mattress ticking is left exposed for the seat and adorned with a quantity of black and white cotton pillows or cushions. Around the base of the frame, white cotton panels are tied at the corners to form a dust skirt .

③ Casual cotton loose-covers an asymmetrical chair.

④ Long, simple ties of co-ordinating fabric add an elegant and attractive finishing touch to a tailored cotton calico cloth that fits perfectly on a small side table in a living room.

③

In contrast, duller, matte textures work better on poor surfaces, as they absorb the light and have the effect of "flattening out" an uneven wall, ceiling or floor area. A rough surface also makes the chosen color seem darker and the overall area appear smaller.

Always try to install the lighting on several different circuits in order to give greater control; if you have the general or background lighting on dimmer switches then part of the room can be dimmed while other features stand out. Other parts of the room may be lit with clear "task" lighting as and when necessary. Attempt to highlight attractive features.

(5) Traditional upholstered armchairs take on a light and modern appearance when loose-covered in fresh white cotton, which is easy to launder.

(6) Unyielding surfaces – in this case a painted concrete floor, a slick tabletop and white plaster walls – provide a good foil for soft furnishings. Here, an antique chair with a well-worn velvet squab cushion stands beside a gilt bench that has been loose-covered with a panel of black cotton and held in place by means of long, knotted ties.

1 Measure the width of the couch or sofa, from the base of one side, up over the arm, across the seat, over the opposite arm and down to the floor again. In this case the measurement was 112 in/284.5 cm.

Measure the depth of the couch or sofa, from the base of the back, over the top, down to the seat, across the seat and down to the floor at the front. In this case the measurement was 102 in/259 cm.

3 Turn in a double ½ in/1.25 cm hem all around and machine down. Miter the corners, see Techniques page 180. Press.

2 Cut out 3 widths of fabric 114 in/289.5 cm long and machine stitch them, long edges together. Trim the overall width evenly on both edges to keep the seams central so that it measures 122 in/310 cm. These measurements include an extra 8 in/20 cm allowance for tucking in at the back; a 5 in/12.5 cm allowance for tucking down at each arm; and a 1 in/2.5 cm seam allowance all around.

LOOSE SOFA COVER
Materials

Basic sewing kit (see page 176)
Approximately 13 yd 5 in/12 m main fabric for a two-seater couch or sofa which is approximately 5 ft/1.5 m long and 3 ft/1 m deep.
The fabric should be 48 in/122 cm wide.

4 Drape the finished panel of fabric right side out over the couch or sofa, tucking in where the seat meets the back and the arms, until there is an even length touching the floor all around the base.

Casual loose covers made of plain cotton lend a feeling of cool comfort in a living room.

5 To make the ties: cut out eight strips of fabric 3 in/7.5 cm wide and 24 in/60 cm long. Fold each strip in half lengthways, right sides together and iron. Fold in the ends ¼ in/0.75 cm and iron. Machine stitch the long open edge of the strip and down one short end.

6 Turn right side out and iron flat. Tuck in and close the open short end with neat hand stitches.

7 Gather the fabric into neat folds at the front of one arm and pin two ties in place. Attach the ties with hand stitches and loosely tie together over the folds. Repeat this for the front of the second arm and twice more where each arm meets the back of the couch or sofa.

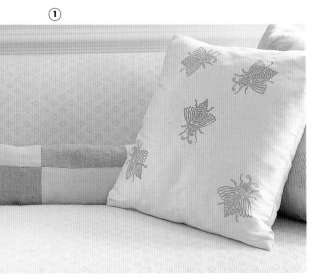

1. Set on a pristine white couch, bee motifs randomly printed on silk sit happily alongside a narrow pillow or cushion that is composed of alternate rectangles of two shades of raw silk.

2. Attractive gilt legs found on antique or reproduction furniture can be left visible by means of a loose cover that does not fall to the floor. Here, the zigzag edging (a detail of the couch in picture 5) is self-bound which adds weight and helps the skirt to hang well.

3. An antique French settee has been elegantly tight-covered in a striped silk rep with close nailing and set off with a contrasting silk bolster and a silk damask pillow or cushion.

4. Black and white cotton appliqué diamonds create a strong impact on a chair in the style of Charles Rennie Mackintosh.

Give prominence to an alcove, a piece of statuary or a flower arrangement. Use accent lighting to give individual features in the room greater impact. Pools of light, thrown by table or floor standard lamps or uplighters illuminate surfaces clearly, add to the overall atmosphere and emphasize the quality of fabrics.

Window, wall and floor treatments, as well as lighting, are all-important in the living room, but upholstered furniture in the form of couches, sofas, chairs, *chaises*, stools, pouffes and ottomans that you actually sit on will probably be the most dominant features. The shapes of the individual pieces of furniture and the way that they are grouped together and positioned alongside tables and other items should be considered in relation to the colors, patterns and textures used for covering. Try to treat the upholstered furniture as an overall composition, although this does not mean that every piece needs to match – different shapes, sizes, styles and materials will add textural interest and contrast of form to the room.

The fabric used for covers need not be uniform, but sometimes covering two disparate pieces will be the only way to unify them.

⑤ In a traditional-style living room, the antique furniture has been smartly upholstered with plenty of white fabric. The whole scheme of the room ties in beautifully. At the windows, the valances or pelmets are made of gathered silk; the seating is upholstered in a heavily woven cotton and the floor is covered with a rich textured wool rug.

⑥ Woven cream jacquard on a couch is set against a wall covered with striped silk.

⑦ Beside a sheer silk drape that bunches elegantly onto a stencilled floor, stands a French settee which is upholstered in a cotton damask with cream trimming. On the settee, a pillow or cushion is given a duo-tone ruffle in gray and cream cotton.

⑧ Cotton damask sits well on an antique French carved couch, see page 4 for a closer view of the fabric.

⑨ A two-color scheme in the corner of a sunny loft or attic; the shapely chair is loose-covered in a white cotton cloth. See picture 8 for a detail of the couch.

⑦

⑧

⑨

1 For the front panel of the cover, measure the height of the inside back of the chair (A), the depth of the chair seat (B) and the width of the chair seat (C). Add an all-around 2½ in/6.25 cm seam allowance. Cut out.

2 For the back panel of the cover, measure the height from the top to the base of the seat (D) and width of the outside back of the chair (E) and add an all-around 1 in/2.5 cm seam allowance. Cut out.

3 For the seat box, measure the length of the front and two sides of the seat; the width of the strip of fabric should be 4 in/10 cm. Add an extra 1 in/2.5 cm seam allowance to all four sides of the strip. Cut out.

4 Measure the front and two sides of the chair seat and cut out a strip of fabric one and a half times the length of this measurement and 8 in/20 cm wide. This strip will form three sides of the skirt.

5 Measure the width of the back of the chair where it joins the seat and cut out a strip of fabric one and a half times the length of this measurement and 8 in/20 cm wide. This strip will form the fourth side of the skirt.

6 Place the front panel of the cover right side up on a flat surface. Lay the 4 in/10 cm wide strip for the seat box cut out in step 3 right side down around three sides of the half panel that will cover the chair seat. Align the raw edges and pin and baste in place. Machine stitch leaving a ½ in/1.25 cm seam allowance. Cut small notches at the corners so that the fabric lies flat. Turn right side out and press.

7 Place the front and back panels right sides together and pin around the top and sides. Slip over the back of the chair to make sure of a loose fit. Cut two small notches in the seam allowance 4 in/10 cm up from the seat to mark the opening at the back.

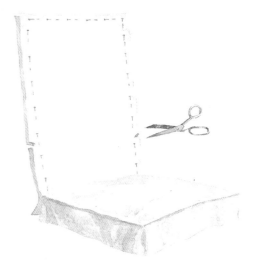

8 Take the pinned fabric panels off the chair and machine together around three sides from notch to notch. Turn right side out and press. Iron a ½ in/1.25 cm fold on the bottom edges of the box seat strip and open out. The fold lines will act as a guide for joining the skirt in steps 11 and 12. Set aside.

9 Take the strip of fabric made in step 4 which will form the front and side skirts of the chair. With the fabric wrong side up, make a double ½ in/1.25 cm fold along the bottom of the strip and press. Fold in both short sides in the same way and press. Machine stitch all the folds.

10 Make a ½ in/1.25 cm fold along the top of the same strip and press. Open out the fold and hand sew along the crease with running stitch, see Techniques page 178. Pull the thread to gather the fabric to the exact length of the front and two sides of the chair seat.

11 To attach the gathered skirt to the box seat, place the whole front panel right side up. Pin and baste the longer strip of gathered skirt to the edge of the seat panel, right side down, following the fold lines made in step 8. Machine right sides together, leaving a ½ in/1.25 cm seam allowance.

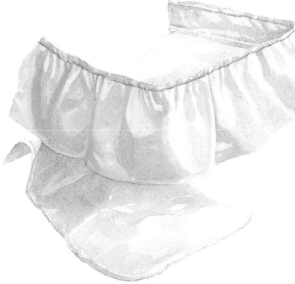

12 Use the same method to attach the shorter strip of gathered skirt to the bottom of the back panel.

13 To make the ties: cut out four strips of fabric each 20 in/50 cm long and 1 ½ in/3.75 cm wide. Fold the sides in ¼ in/0.75 cm all around. Miter the corners, see Techniques page 180, and press.

Fold in half lengthways, right sides together and machine around the outer edge.

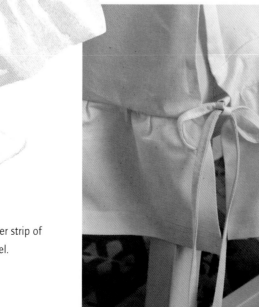

LOOSE OCCASIONAL CHAIR COVER

Materials

Basic sewing kit (see page 176)
Approximately 5 ft/1.5 m fabric per chair
Upright wooden chair

A cream-painted wooden chair is loose-covered in cotton duck and fastened with ties.

14 Hand sew the two openings at the back of the chair with a neat hemming stitch, see Techniques page 178. Attach two ties with hand stitches to each opening where the back and side skirts meet.

①

Different fabrics, some plain, some patterned, perhaps with checks and stripes to act as a link, will be much more interesting and will add character to a room – so long as they come from the same color palette. You can work clever juxtapositions with pillows or cushions, trimmings, valances or pelmets and pipings in order to marry the various items together. There are all sorts of ways of dressing a chair or couch, from tightly tailored covers to more casual treatments such as baggy loose covers or slip covers or casual throws. Covers can then be trimmed in a variety of ways, using neat piping, deep fringing, frilled valances or pelmets and decorative braids.

Making a loose cover involves more of a "couture" approach. The traditional way that a dress designer works is to use a *toile* in muslin or calico or another kind of basic cloth in order to test the cut and line, without being influenced by the texture and pattern of the final fabric. You can use this technique yourself to make patterns and to test the shape and overall effect, not only with upholstered furniture but also with window treatments, bed and table covers – in fact the whole gamut of soft furnishings. This might seem time-wasting if you are planning to use an inexpensive fabric, but if you are going to use an expensive, exotic textile this method could help you to avoid a costly mistake.

Apart from the look of the fabric you will need to consider its practical aspects. Aside from choosing a fabric which is easily washable, shrink-, stain- and snag-resistant and needs little ironing, any trimmings should be color-fast and fastenings must be rust- and launder-proof; you also need to think about softness and drapeability. This is almost as important a consideration when deciding on fabric for covering furniture as it is for making drapes or curtains.

(1) Strong, architectural shapes are the key to this scheme. An oval sisal rug with a stencilled border, panelled white walls and exaggerated upholstered shapes combine to provide a classical modern style. A mix of pastel silks softens the upholstery.

(2) The rigidity of a box-shaped buttoned *chaise longue* is broken with a mound of pale pillows or cushions.

(3) Kick pleats neaten the corners of a cream damask loose-covered chair.

(4) Simple furnishings contribute to the sense of space in a large room. In this living room light colors abound: the upholstered couch has deep fringing and sheer silk drapes suspended from a painted pole allow maximum daylight to penetrate. The stencilled sisal rug on the floor adds an interesting circular outline to a room dominated by straight lines.

(5) The contemporary lines of a light wood chair are highlighted with linen upholstery.

(6) In a townhouse living room a sheer Roman shade or blind helps to diffuse strong sunlight. The parquet floor is softened with a hand-tufted wool rug which echoes the pale wood seating and neutral upholstery.

①

③ ④

②

Throws and looser treatments, such as baggy loose covers cry out for malleable textiles which fall in soft folds, but fabric must be much more firmly woven for tight covers. Wearability is another important factor – taffetas and silks look delightful at windows but they are rarely strong enough for even the loosest cover, although they are suitable for pillow or cushion covers. Pure linen is certainly a beautiful fabric to use for soft furnishings but because it crumples easily when sat on it may be more appropriate for drapes or pillows or cushions rather than upholstery.

Flammability is another essential factor to consider when choosing fabrics for the home. There are rules and regulations which govern

⑤

⑥

① A button-back slipper chair is upholstered in fine beige wool and the kick-pleated skirt is held in place with close nailing.

② Camel-hair wool is a cozy soft furnishing fabric. This child's chair has a tailored floor-length skirt and a matching pillow or cushion.

③④ Soft browns and beige give this family room a warm and inviting ambience. The self-piped chair and couch are upholstered in camel-hair wool and sit well on the heavily woven jute matting on the floor.

⑤ Traditional upholstery is strengthened by webbing. Here, interwoven tapestry fabric simulates colorful webbing and is left exposed for decorative effect at the back of a French *fauteuil* chair.

⑥ Clusters of pearls sewn by hand onto a cream linen pillow or cushion. The velvet chenille throw draped on the arm of the couch adds a touch of luxury.

⑦ Positioned in the corner of a formal living room, a crescent-shaped couch covered in silk sweeps around a circular occasional table. Its elegance is enhanced by deep box pleats around the skirt and softly tucked pleats on the arms.

⑦

the use of fabrics for tight covers and upholstery and such fabrics have to be either back-coated or dipped in a special solution if they are not inherently flameproof; some fabrics such as wool are naturally slow to ignite. Note that some inflammable fabrics may be stiff and uncomfortable to sit on or relax against, while you can make more supple types of texture flameproof by inserting a barrier cloth in between the filling and the top fabric. In the main, proper furnishing fabrics are recommended for upholstery and fitted covers – these will have passed a rub test, for wear and tear, and also a cigarette and match test, giving them a fire rating specification. However, some dress

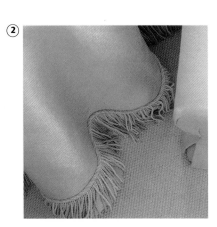

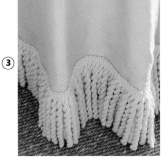

fabrics are tough enough to use for fitted and loose covers, denim for example, and some woven woollen fabrics such as flannel, worsted and firmly woven tweed – although none of these would pass the above tests. Dressmaking fabrics may be suitable for some of the baggy loose or slip covers or throws, so long as you don't expect them to last for years. In fact, part of their charm is that they can be changed depending on the time of year or to provide a change of scene. Dressmaking fabrics will not be flameproof and they are much more likely to fade than furnishing types.

Practicalities aside, you will want to choose a fabric based on aesthetics – should it be patterned or plain, printed or woven, smooth or heavily textured, floral or geometric, striped or checked or a specific period-style fabric? All too often convention steps in – Chippendale-style chairs are upholstered in woven Regency stripes, even though this fabric was not used in the days of the Regent; *chaises longues* are covered in velvet, plush or similar stripes; Chesterfields, wing and club elbow- or armchairs are encased in leather and a Knole couch or sofa receives a self-colored brocade or damask cover. Yet it is possible to use fabrics in much more exciting ways than these. For instance, a day-bed or *chaise* can look wonderful in plain, solid and bright colors, mattress ticking, a tartan or a fabric with a strong Oriental flavor or even a mini-print floral with a companion border print used to frame the contours and echoed in bolsters, pillows or cushions at each end. A Chesterfield looks much less crouching covered in a light, pretty fabric – florals work well but avoid checks or stripes because the heavy buttoning can distort the pattern. Club or

smarter fabric such as wide canvas stripes in strong, plain colors piped to contrast and outline the shape, bold Paisley prints or a traditional geometric. Of course, if you do have a conservatory then floral covers for your cane furniture are quite in keeping – try to create a link with the view beyond the glass, perhaps echoing the blooms in the garden or a pattern used on patio furniture.

Visualizing the finished effect of a pattern on furniture can be difficult, especially if you are ordering a couch or a chair which you may have seen covered in one fabric and you intend to use a totally different one. This is hard enough with loose covers, but a mistake can be changed more easily than with tight upholstery where an error of judgment is more serious. Try to disassociate yourself from the cover in place.

wing elbow- or armchairs can be smartly upholstered in a tweed and Knole couches take on a whole new personality if given a Scottish baronial treatment with a tartan cover. Regency-style chairs, which have a wooden frame and a padded back and seat, can be given a "mix-and-match" treatment: the seat and inside back could have a formal floral *petit point* cover and the outer back could be done in a companion plain fabric, a check or stripe. This different treatment for the back works well with many wood-framed chairs and those which incorporate cane on the sides or arms. You could upholster one couch in a tartan fabric and another in a companion stripe, giving two possible themes to echo in the chair backs or seats. Pillows or cushions in both fabrics, with plain piping, will co-ordinate the seating further.

Cane couches and other seats can be made to look much more luxurious and also be made much more comfortable to sit on with the addition of boxed squab cushions. Avoid using a floral fabric as this may give the impression of conservatory cast-offs; instead dress them in

1. Four antique prints hung close together provide a classical backdrop for a skirted silk tablecloth.
2. Occasional tablecloths can be given decorative finishing touches by sewing a trim around the perimeter. This raw silk cloth is embellished with a deep fringe which rests on a beige flat-weave rug.
3. A silk tablecloth fringed with mercerized cotton.
4. A harmonious combination of fabrics gives this living room a sophisticated feel. Rich, raw silk drapes can be drawn over light-diffusing woven cream roller shades or blinds. The neutral fabrics on the upholstered furniture provide a variety of textures to avoid uniformity. The carpet is a mix of beige jute and wool.
5. A bright floral fabric tablecloth with tailored corners sits happily in betweeen a pair of chairs which have seats upholstered in cotton ticking.
6. Printed linen drapes are finished with a thick cotton fringe which has been sewn to round off the corners.
7. Beside a rich cream chenille couch and a matching armchair, an ornately printed linen tablecloth creates an elegant impression and the cloth is edged in a cotton rope border.

1 Measure up a panel of main fabric according to the dimensions of the inside back of the chair. Make sure that the grain is straight and the pattern square. Cut out the fabric 4 in/10 cm larger all around and use T-pins (these are extra long pins with T-bars or large heads which are easier to handle than normal pins) to pin the panel to the chair, right side out, centering the pattern and smoothing the fabric out toward the edges. Once the fabric is pinned in place, trim the edges so that there is a ½ in/1.25 cm seam allowance around the top and sides and a 4 in/10 cm allowance along the bottom where the back meets the seat – this is for tucking in.

2 Remove the inside back panel from the chair by taking out the pins. Cut three vertical slits at regular intervals along the bottom 4 in/10 cm allowance. Each slit should be 3¼ in/8 cm long. Then cut out three triangular pieces from your main fabric, each should measure 1½ in/3.75 cm along the bottom edge and the other two equal sides should measure 3½ in/8.75 cm.

3 Place each triangular piece of fabric right side down and make a ¼ in/0.75 cm fold around all three sides. Press. Working right side up, machine stitch the folds.

4 Pin a triangle over each of the slits made in step 2 and machine the two long sides of each triangle to each side of each slit, work with the fabric right side up. Pin the whole panel with T-pins to the chair again, right side up.

To fit the loose cover, accurate measuring is required. For each panel that makes up the cover, first measure the area of the chair to be covered and add an allowance for pinning to the chair and trimming sufficient seam allowances. These vary according to the individual panels. When each panel is pinned in place, then cut accurately to size, working on the chair.

5 For the arms: measure up two panels of main fabric according to the dimensions of the inside and front of the arms of the chair. Cut out both panels of fabric 4 in/10 cm larger all around and pin each panel to the chair arms, with T-pins, right side out, centering the pattern. At the front of each arm pin a dart at the corner, (see step 16 to finish the dart). Once the two arm panels are pinned in place, trim the edges to a ½ in/1.25 cm seam allowance around all sides except the edge adjacent to the seat. On the bottom edge allow a 4 in/10cm allowance for tucking in. Leave the arm panels pinned to the chair.

LOOSE WING CHAIR COVER

Materials

Basic sewing kit (see page 176)
Approximately 5 yd 20 in/6 m main fabric
5 yd 20 in/6 m made-up piping in contrasting fabric
(see Techniques, page 181)
Plenty of T-pins and ordinary pins Tailor's chalk
11 yd/10 m cotton tape
1 yd/1 m contrasting fabric

6 For the seat: measure up a panel of main fabric according to the dimensions of the seat. Make sure that the grain is vertical and the pattern square. Cut out a panel of fabric 4 in/10 cm larger all around and pin the fabric to the seat with T-pins, right side out, centering the pattern. Trim the edges so that there is a ½ in/1.25 cm seam allowance along the front edge of the panel and a 4 in/10 cm allowance for tucking in around the sides and back. Leave the seat panel pinned to the chair.

7 For the front of the chair seat: measure up a panel of main fabric according to the dimensions of the front of the chair below the seat. Make sure that the grain is vertical and the pattern square. Cut out a panel of main fabric  4 in/10 cm larger all around and pin the fabric to the chair with T-pins, right side out, centering the pattern. Trim the edges so that there is a ½ in/1.25 cm seam allowance around the top and sides and a 3 in/7.5 cm allowance along the bottom for turning under the chair. Leave this panel pinned to the chair.

8 For the outside back and arms of the chair: measure up two symmetrical panels of equal size according to the dimensions of half the back and one outside arm of the chair. Cut out two panels of main fabric 6 in/15 cm larger all around and pin the fabric to the chair with T-pins, right side out, centering the pattern. On one back panel, allow an extra 4 in/10 cm along the straight edge (for a neat overlap) which runs down the middle of the chair back, plus a ½ in/1.25 cm seam allowance all around the curved top and arm edge and a 3 in/7.5 cm allowance for turning under the chair along the bottom edge. Leave this panel pinned to the chair.

9 Pin the other half of the outside back and arm panel to the chair with T-pins, aligning the pattern. Add a 6 in/15 cm seam allowance along the straight edge which runs down the middle of the back, plus a ½ in/1.25 cm seam allowance all around the curved top and arm edge and a 3 in/7.5 cm allowance for turning under the chair along the bottom edge. Make a 2 in/5 cm fold along the straight edge down the middle of the back on this second back panel and pin the fold in place. The overlap down the middle of the back should now measure 4 in/10cm – this will form the opening to the chair cover. Leave this second back panel pinned to the chair.

10 With all the panels still pinned to the chair with T-pins, mark the seam lines that will join all parts of the loose cover by pinning the seam allowances together all over the chair with ordinary pins. When all the ordinary pins are in place and the cover fits the chair perfectly, mark the seam lines by opening out the seam allowances with your fingers. Mark the wrong side of the fabric inside the crease of the seam with tailor's chalk. Leave the ordinary pins in place. Cut a series of small, triangular notches through both layers of all the adjoining ½ in/1.25 cm seam allowances at roughly 4 in/10 cm intervals. Do this all the way around the chair, along all the raw edges.

11 Next, remove the T-pins which are still holding the seven separate fabric panels to the body of the chair. The ordinary pins, the tailor's chalk outline and the series of notches all serve as a seam guide for sewing the panels together once the cover is removed from the chair.

12 Remove all the T-pins and lift the whole cover off the chair. In order to seam the edges of the panels together, work around the pinned seam lines and invert all the raw edges. To do this, remove the pins one by one along the seam allowance, invert the seam allowance and re-pin in place on the wrong side of the fabric. Continue to turn the whole cover wrong side out, pinning accurately along the line of tailor's chalk and aligning the notches as a guide. Once the whole loose cover is wrong-side out it is ready for seaming.

13 Working with all the joined panels of fabric wrong side out, baste along all the pinned seam lines which will not be finished with corded piping – in other words, all the seams except the one which runs across the front of the seat and the long shaped seam which runs from one front leg up the adjoining arm, around the back and down the opposite arm to the opposite front leg, see the main photograph. Machine stitch along the basting line, lining up the notches.

14 Make up 5 yd 20 in/6 m of corded piping, see Techniques page 181. Insert the piping in between panels pinned together so that it will lie along the front of the seat and around the perimeter of the arms, sides and top of the chair (see the main photograph). To do this, work with the fabric right sides together, remove a few pins at a time and insert the raw edge of the piping in between the two layers of main fabric which are right sides together. Position the piping exactly along the line of pins and re-pin all the raw edges together ½ in/1.25 cm in from the edge. Continue until all the piping is pinned in place. Baste the two layers of fabric and piping along the line of pins and remove the pins. Make small snips in the raw edges around curves or corners to make sure of a neat fit.

15 Working on the wrong side of the fabric, machine along the line of basting stitches, lining up the notches. Leaving a ½ in/1.25 cm seam allowance all around, machine stitch close to the piping cord.

16 For the darts on the front edge of the arms, machine stitch along the dart line pinned in step 5 on the wrong side of the fabric. Trim the excess fabric and overlock the raw edges to prevent fraying, see Techniques page 180.

17 Turn the whole cover right side out and press. To finish the opening at the back of the chair: fold and pin the long inner straight edge into a double 1 in/2.5 cm hem. Turn the existing outer fold made in step 9 under to make a double 1 in/2.5 cm hem. Hand sew both straight edges with neat hemming stitch. Press. Slip the cover over the chair and tuck in the flaps around the sides and back of the seat.

18 At each leg, trim the fabric so that there is a ¾ in/2 cm hem allowance. To finish the legs, see step 21.

19 Turn the chair on its back and working on the underside, pinch the allowance of fabric tight and pin a series of 3 in/7.5 cm darts to turn under all around the front, sides and back of the chair.

20 Remove the cover from the chair and turn in ½ in/1.25 cm all around the allowance of fabric for the underside of the chair. Iron the turn-in and machine stitch to prevent fraying. Hand sew along the darts also.

21 At all four legs, make a cut as shown. Turn the fabric under a further ½ in /1.25 cm and hem neatly by hand.

22 Working on the underside of the chair cover, take the binding tape and hand sew 13 .loops, each about ¾ in/2 cm long at regular intervals to the edge of the turn-under allowance. Place the cover back on the chair.

23 Take a long piece of binding tape and string it through all 13 loops in a cross-over pattern. Pull the tape taut and tie in a bow. This will give the bottom edge of the cover a neat, wrinkle-free finish.

24 To close the opening down the middle of the back of the chair: measure up ten strips of contrasting fabric, each 12 in/30 cm long and 2½ in/6.25 cm wide. Cut out. Fold each strip in half lengthways, right sides together, and machine along the long side and one short end ½ in /1.25 cm in from the edge. With the blunt end of a pencil, turn each strip right side out. Press. Tuck in the open end and hand stitch neatly to close.

Hand sew the five pairs of ties to either side of the back flaps of the cover at regular intervals, finishing with a pair right at the bottom of the opening. Tie each pair of ties into a bow.

An antique wing chair is given a smart treatment with a tailored loose cover made of printed linen and closed at the back by means of ties.

Instead, look at the whole form of the piece of furniture, preferably in a plain cover and try to work out how an alternative pattern will "sit" on the back, seat and arms. If possible, obtain a large sample of the fabric that you like and drape it over the couch or chair in order to help visualize the whole design.

The first factor to consider when choosing a patterned fabric is the size and scale of the design. You should relate the scale of the pattern to the size of the surface on which it is to be used. Next think about the form of the piece of furniture – flowing florals can look good on more curvaceous items and can also soften a very square design. While checks, stripes and geometrics may present the problem of neat alignment over a scroll arm or curved back. Any bold pattern must be centered on the back of a couch or chair and a design with a clear "direction" must be followed through over the seat pillows or cushions and over the arms. The pattern on a valance or pleated base must also line up; with a strong directional pattern matching up may be virtually impossible or else very costly so the

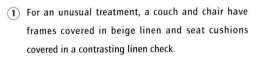

(1) For an unusual treatment, a couch and chair have frames covered in beige linen and seat cushions covered in a contrasting linen check.

(2) A detail of the throw in picture 1 shows strips of handwoven linen in a checkerboard pattern.

(3) Subtle woven checked linen covers a tailored couch.

(4) On a couch corner a cotton matelasse kick pleat is edged in self-binding. A linen throw rests on the arm.

(5) Set against a background of panelled walls and a dark wood floor a pair of large couches are loose-covered in a cotton matelasse and provide generous seating around a sawbuck table.

alternative is to use a plain toning base trim. In some cases, positioning a large, bold motif in the middle of plain back and seat pillows or cushions is a good solution and also one which involves less wastage of fabric. It is equally important for the lines in checked, striped and plaid materials to meet accurately at the seams. With loose covers you will have to try them on the furniture to test for pattern matching, but if you are going to make your own then it is prudent to use a plain fabric for a first attempt and then graduate to simple, non-directional patterns before advancing to stripes or checks. Reserve large, bold patterns until you become more experienced and proficient.

Loose covers are an ideal way of extending the life of permanent covers, changing the color scheme or providing a seasonal change, but they should not be used as an inexpensive form of re-upholstery because they will not disguise sagging springs or lumpy padding. In fact, loose springs can work their way through to the top surface and may well cut through the loose cover fabric. This type of cover is made in sections. Large rectangles which correspond to those of the original upholstery cover are seamed together with a fabric "tuck-in" allowance; in some cases two pieces of fabric may have to be seamed to make one of the sections. The "tuck-in" allowance is added to the appropriate edges of the rectangular sections so that they can be tucked into the crevices around the seat and help to anchor the cover in position and prevent strain. The bottom edges of the cover may be made with flaps which tie underneath the chair or couch for a neat, tight finish. As an alternative, the cover can be finished with a "skirt" with corner kick pleats or a frilled or box-pleated valance. Piping the seams also helps to prevent strain and forms a break in between the joined sections and it can also be used as a decorative feature to contrast or co-ordinate with the main cover and to define the shape of the piece.

There are various paper patterns available for making loose covers, but as with stretch and ready-made loose covers the fit is rarely accurate enough for your couches and chairs! It is far better to make your own loose covers by cutting each piece of fabric to fit the overall dimensions of the item of furniture, pinning the pieces together and fitting them onto the piece, adjusting as necessary. To work out how much fabric you need requires careful measuring and you must work to a cutting plan. You can then work out the number and size of the pieces needed – the ideal way to do this is to use graph paper so that your measurements are correct.

You can make a *toile*, or a trial cover, from a length of inexpensive fabric such as discarded sheeting, curtain or drape lining, muslin or calico or cotton. Test this out first on the piece of furniture and adjust the fit. You will then need to unpick your *toile* and use it as the pattern for the real cover. And if you already have loose covers on the furniture which you wish to discard then you can use these as a guide, unpicking them if necessary. When you cut out the actual pieces you will need plenty of space to lay out the fabric with the cutting plan laid on top. If you

① Under a staircase, an occasional table with angled sides is covered with a tailored cloth. Panels of red and white linen checks are edged in a smaller check sewn on the cross and the kick pleats are made from the same diminutive check.

② Plenty of dark navy and white cotton checks dominate a family living room which is situated just off a spacious kitchen. The large, box-shaped couch, chairs and stool echo the window treatments and the strong geometric upholstery is broken up by a few tartan and contrasting check pillows or cushions.

③ A cotton check loose cover which is fastened by knotted ties dresses a small, slope-backed chair and features piped skirted panels.

④ Ordinary black and white mattress ticking makes a smart tight cover for a button-backed chair.

⑤ The "buttons" on the same chair are in fact exquisite miniature bows made of ticking fabric.

⑥ Fresh blue and white checked linen provides a smart loose cover for an armchair. The pillow or cushion is fashioned from pieces of felt that have been cut into intricate shapes and appliquéd by hand onto a contrasting backing fabric.

⑦ Instead of traditional piping, this red and white woven linen pillow or cushion with knife pleat corners is trimmed with flat piping. A wider strip of fabric has been doubled over and used on the cross.

⑧ Wicker furniture in the living area shown in picture 9 is upholstered in fresh striped linen and trimmed with traditional piping.

③

④
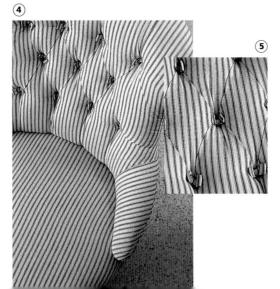

⑤

⑨ In an informal country-style living area, red and white fabrics contrast boldly with a huge pine server or dresser that is laden with a collection of blue and white china. Large wicker chairs and a couch are upholstered in cheerful linen and a collection of antique *toile de Jouy* pillows or cushions break up the stripes and checks. At the window, checked cotton drapes hang simply from a thin black iron rod and rings and echo the room's color scheme.

⑥

don't have access to a large table or trestle then you can use the floor, but make sure that it is clean, absolutely flat and that you don't damage the surface underneath. Use sharp dressmaking or upholstery scissors. Once cut, you will find that all the pieces look the same, so in order to prevent muddling them up, attaach a small sticky label to the wrong side of the fabric stating which piece is which and the direction that each should be placed on the couch or chair. This is particularly helpful if you are using a pile fabric as all the nap should face the same way; with a patterned fabric the design should match throughout and it must all be set on the piece of furniture in the same direction.

Accessories come into their own in the living room. Here you can add personal touches to enhance your scheme and introduce extra visual interest, textural and tonal contrast and sharp accent colors. Antique textiles can be displayed by incorporating them into the scheme as cloths, pillows or cushions and hangings or they may be combined with or backed by a modern fabric, which should be of a suitable weight to support the older piece.

Take care with fragile fabrics – these may need to be sewn onto a backing and may only be suitable mounted under glass, perhaps on top of a table with a plate-glass top, or framed as a picture. If in doubt about the correct treatment for a valuable old piece of embroidery, woven textile or delicate patchwork of silk pieces you

should seek the advice of an expert fabric restorer. Old kelims and other rugs or pieces of durable fabric which are worn and no longer suitable for use on the floor can be recycled as attractive wall hangings, or they might be cut and the good part made into pillows or cushions or used to upholster a small stool or chair. However, do not cut a valuable Oriental or any other type of rug into pieces when it might be better restored and returned to its former glory; again you should seek the advice of an expert before getting out the scissors.

APPLIQUE SLIPPER CHAIR COVER

Materials

Basic sewing kit (see page 176)
5 yd /4.5 m main checked fabric
2 yd 26 in/2.5 m appliqué floral fabric
Piping cord
2 yd 7 in/2 m contrasting fabric for binding and piping
Embroidery thread in contrasting color
Embroidery needle

1 For the back panel: measure the height of the chair from the top of the back to the floor (A). Measure the width of the back of the chair (B).

2 Add ½ in/1.25 cm to A and 8 in/20 cm to B for seam allowances. Cut out a panel of main checked fabric to these dimensions. Cut the panel down the middle. (Note, if you are using fabric with a large pattern repeat, increase the width of the panel to allow for pattern matching.)

3 Lay the two panels wrong side up on a flat surface, making sure that the checks align. Fold back the two long inside edges 2 in/5 cm and press.
Machine stitch down the crease 6 in/15 cm from the top edge to join the panels. Press open the seam.

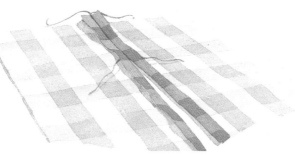

4 Working wrong side up, fold in 1 in/2.5 cm double hem down both seam allowances in the middle of the panel. Hem neatly by hand, see Techniques page 178.

5 Fold the central, hemmed join at the top of the panel into a flap and press to the right side. Baste along the top to hold in position.

A slipper chair, loose-covered in a checked linen with a panel of printed chintz that has been blanket-stitched around the skirt and across the top.

6 For the front panel: measure the length of the inside seat back and across the seat (C); add 2 in/5 cm to tuck the fabric in where the seat meets the back. Measure the width across the inside seat back (D). Add ½ in/1.25 cm seam allowance all around this panel and cut out a piece of main checked fabric to these dimensions. Set aside.

7 For the skirt: measure the two sides and front of the chair seat (E) and measure the drop for the skirt from the top of the seat to the floor (F). Add ½ in/1.25 cm seam allowance to the sides and top of the panel. Cut out a piece of main checked fabric to these dimensions. Set aside.

8 For the inset corner panels at the back of the chair: measure the length from under the seat to the floor (G). The width of each panel is 6 in/15 cm. Cut out two panels of appliqué fabric to these dimensions. Set aside.

9 Make up 6 yd 20 in/6 m of corded piping from the contrasting fabric, see Techniques page 181. Set aside.

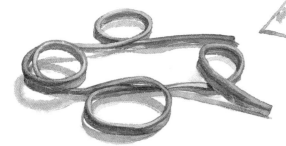

10 Make up enough binding in contrasting fabric to trim the bottom of the skirt and the two corner inset panels. To do this, cut out a strip of contrasting fabric 4 yd 14 in/4 m long and 2 in/5 cm wide. Join strips where necessary, see Techniques page 181. Set aside.

11 To make the ties for the back of the chair: cut out six strips of contrasting fabric, each one 6 in/15 cm long and 1¼ in/3 cm wide. Place the strip right side down and fold in all the edges by ¼ in/0.75 cm. Make a 45° angle at each end. Press the folded edges and machine stitch. Repeat for six ties. Set aside.

12 For the appliqué: measure up a panel of appliqué fabric the length of the skirt (E); the panel can be as deep as you like. Measure up a second panel to the width of the top of the chair back (D); this can be as deep as you like. Measure up two more pieces to the width of the two back skirt panels (half of B). On each of these panels, add an extra ½ in/1.25 cm seam allowance at the sides only. Cut out all the panels.

13 Depending on the pattern of the appliqué fabric, cut out a shaped outline as required. In this case the outline follows the floral design.

14 For the skirt: lay the panel of checked fabric cut out in step 7 right side up on a flat surface. Lay the appliqué panel cut out in step 12 over it, also right side up. Align the bottom and side edges and pin and baste together.

15 With an embroidery needle and embroidery thread, blanket stitch, see Techniques page 179, the shaped outline of appliqué to the checked panel.

16 For the inside top of the chair: lay the front panel of checked fabric cut out in step 6 right side up on a flat surface. Lay the appliqué panel cut out in step 12 over it, also right side up. Align the top and side edges and pin and baste together. Blanket stitch the shaped outline as in step 15.

17 For the back skirt: lay the back panel made in step 5 right side up on a flat surface. Lay the two appliqué panels cut out in step 12 over each half of the bottom of the panel, also right side up. Align the bottom and side edges and pin and baste together. Blanket stitch the shaped outline as in step 15. The shaped outline of the appliqué on the skirt should align all around. Fold in and press the seam allowance in the middle to neaten both sides of the opening. Hem neatly by hand on the underside. Set aside.

18 To sew the piping to the back panel: lay the whole panel right side up on a flat surface. Place the piping made in step 9 around two sides and the top, ½ in/1.25 cm in from the raw edge. Pin and baste in place. The raw edges of the piping and the panel should all face outward. Machine outside the cord around all three sides. Make a diagonal snip at both top corners for a rounded edge. Set aside.

19 To sew the skirt to the front panel: lay the front panel wrong side up and pin and baste three sides of the skirt around the end without the appliqué, leaving a ½ in/1.25 cm seam allowance. Machine the skirt to the seat, right sides together, easing around the corners. Turn right side out and press.

20 To sew the back panel to the front panel: place both panels right sides together, aligning the top and sides. Pin and baste together. Machine stitch outside the piping sewn to the back panel in step 17, leaving a ½ in/1.25 seam allowance. Machine stitch around the top and down both sides, stopping where the appliqué on the skirt begins. Make sure that all the raw edges are pointing outward. Turn right side out and press.

21 Pin, baste and machine stitch a length of corded piping to the two untrimmed edges of the skirt, stitching along the ½ in/1.25 seam allowance. Press and trim off any excess raw edges.

22 Take the two panels of appliqué fabric previously cut out in step 8. Overlock, see Techniques page180, all four sides on both pieces, without folding the edges. This will prevent fraying.

23 Working on the skirt, place the back and side panels of the skirt right side down, leaving the corner as a V-shaped slit. Place one panel of appliqué right side down centered over the opening so that the top edge overlaps the top of the slit by ½ in/1.25 cm. Hand sew neatly

along the top edge into the inside layer of the skirt so that the stitches will not be visible from the right side. Repeat for the second back corner.

24 To sew the binding around the base of the skirt: lay the strips prepared in step 10 along the right side of the bottom of the skirt. Machine stitch ½ in/1.25 cm up from the bottom edge.

25 Turn down the 1½ in/3.75 cm of binding that remains above the seam line and fold under the bottom of the skirt to enclose the raw edge. Make a double ½ in/1.25 cm fold on the reverse side of the skirt. Pin and baste in place. Hem the binding around the wrong side of the bottom edge of the skirt. Sew binding to the bottom edge of the two corner inset panels separately.

26 Take the six ties made in step 11 and hand sew neatly in three pairs down the back of the chair, to close the back cover. Tie into bows.

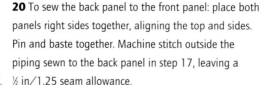

Pillows or cushions and bolsters of all types, shapes and sizes can be piled onto chairs, sofas, window seats, day beds, *chaises* and ottomans and will often provide a useful means of tying various different upholstered pieces together, or of linking the drape or curtain fabric into the overall scheme of a room. Always buy enough fabric when making drapes or curtains and covers so that you have some left over to cover one or two pillows or cushions.

In some rooms these will be important items – they may be large, firm and used to sink into, perhaps providing extra seating or floor pillows or cushions. In other instances they may be more incidental, with an appliqué, hand-embroidered or decorative machine-stitched design, or used to add a touch of frivolity or luxury. Whatever your choice, you should always consider the practical aspects of the fabric and make sure that the covers are easy to remove and suitable for cleaning.

Lamps and shades are other important accessories in the living room. They can be added as a final touch in addition to the main lighting, Shades for wall lights and pendants provide decorative finishing touches and should tie in with the overall theme of the room in style and color. For a host of ideas for making pillows or cushions and lampshades, see the Accessories chapter on pages 148-73.

① In a cottage living room an early 20th-century *chaise longue* is covered in a hard-wearing woven linen and viscose plaid. An ordinary knotted cotton sheet provides an instant tablecloth and blue and white cotton rugs adorn the floor.

② An overscaled chair upholstered in cream linen is placed in a sunny corner beside a dormer window. The back and seat of the chair are given a practical treatment with panels of dark-blue linen edged in a check. Fastened with ties, these are easy to remove for cleaning. At the window, the drape has been lengthened by sewing a strip of blue crocheted lace in between two panels of checked cotton.

③ Small detachable panels of hemmed fabric with knotted ties are useful for protecting seating from wear and tear. Here, even the arm of a chair is loose-covered with a printed linen.

④⑤ A painted black Chinese bamboo chair is softened with a diamond quilted *toile de Jouy* squab cushion which is buttoned with cotton tufts. The wall behind is covered in co-ordinating fabric and a white cotton rug with a linen fringe lies on the sisal floor.

85

THE DINING ROOM may be a separate, single-purpose room or a less formal area which is part of the kitchen or adjoins the living room. You may have a separate dining room for formal entertaining and important family occasions and use the kitchen for day-to-day meals. Whatever the arrangement, these rooms are where family and friends gather together to share meals and so it is fitting to choose soft furnishings which are inviting and comfortable, as well as practical in a food environment.

If the dining area is an extension of the kitchen or living room you will need to link the two areas visually and integrate the color scheme throughout. You can add extra touches in your table setting and echo these in accessories in other parts of the room – this is particularly important when the kitchen and dining area are linked as kitchens tend to have a cool atmosphere because of a predominance of shiny textures such as cabinets, tiles and work counters. For example, a rich terra-cotta or apricot tablecloth and napkins and a copper pendant lamp in the dining room can be reflected by earthenware pots filled with herbs and copper pans in the kitchen; or a cheerful red and white checked dining cloth with co-ordinating napkins and squab cushions might be repeated in café curtains in the kitchen. In the same way, sunny yellow walls for the whole area can be teamed with blue cooking utensils and pottery in the kitchen and a yellow and blue patterned fabric used for table and seat covers and window treatments in both areas will serve to unify the two. In a combined dining and living area try to co-ordinate furnishings to some degree, for instance a rose-pink table cover could be used in close proximity to a traditional living room decorated in a cool scheme with the warmer rose echoed in pillows or cushions, as piping on a couch or chairs and as the dominant color in a floral drape fabric. The possibilities of mixing and matching colors in neighboring schemes are endless and the whole matter of combining colors is, of course, highly subjective.

Whatever fabric you decide to use, consider that eating areas need regular cleaning. Keep a practical eye on chair covers and upholstery, which need to be hard-wearing and easy-care. Make sure that fabrics have been treated so that they are stain- and shrink-resistant and also fade-proof and consider the benefits of chairs with tie-on squabs or slip-on covers which can easily be removed for washing.

Dining rooms and kitchens

Opposite A set of loose-covered dining-room chairs; the short, gathered skirts are made of washable cotton piqué and are held in place with ties.

(1)(2) A sculptured metal table and clean-lined wood chairs are set against a somewhat austere panelled wall. The chairs are upholstered in a pale woven harlequin cotton, which is sparingly mitered at the corners.

(3) In a dining room, the chairs have woven backs and the seats are upholstered in a tiny woven check. The check theme and the square-panelled walls are echoed in the drapes.

(4) At the window, the squared pattern in the drapes mirrors the wall panelling. Two pale shades of silk squares are sewn together and hang from wooden rings on a pole.

(4)

(1)

(2)

(3)

Where the dining area is part of the kitchen or if the seating is often used by children, then it is preferable for chairs to be of solid wood with rush seats or tie-on squab cushions. It is also useful to have a spare set of squabs.

Two additional factors will contribute to the overall impression of the scheme – lighting and flooring. In the dining room the table should be softly lit. Candlelight at the table creates a friendly ambience. In the kitchen lighting should be designed for efficient food preparation rather than ambience. If you decide on a hard flooring for a dual-purpose dining room then you can soften the sitting area with a rug or rush matting under the table. If you prefer a carpet then choose one which will not show stains caused by spilt food or drink. Suitable types include those with a small motif or a slightly mottled or tweedy look, a hard-twist pile, an easy-care fiber content and a stain-resistant finish. In combined kitchens and dinings rooms or in heavily used dining rooms textiles need to be highly practical.

(5) Silk panels of pale pink and cream have been used to upholster an antique French settee, while the reproduction black ebonized wood chairs have cotton sateen squabs with whimsical black appliqué motifs.

(6) Lemon-yellow and cream squares of cotton poplin are sewn together in a patchwork to cover the table.

(7)(8) A plain, oval-backed dining chair is given an elegant loose cover in cotton rep and piped in a strong contrasting color.

1 Cut out a piece of fabric for the table top; in this case the panel measured 61 in/152.5 cm x 37 in/92.5 cm, allowing 1 in/2.5 cm seam allowance all around.

2 For the skirt: cut out six widths of fabric each 32 in/80 cm deep. (Two for each side and one for each end of the table.)

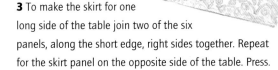

3 To make the skirt for one long side of the table join two of the six panels, along the short edge, right sides together. Repeat for the skirt panel on the opposite side of the table. Press.

4 To make the middle box pleat place the two joined panels right side up on a flat surface. With the seam in the middle, fold a double pleat measuring 4 in/10 cm to the left of the seam and a double pleat also measuring 4 in/10 cm to the right of the seam. Press.

5 To secure each box pleat: lay the pleated panel flat, right side up. Fold the right-hand pleat over to the left. Machine stitch 3 in/7.5 cm down the central crease and open the pleat to the right as before. Repeat for the left-hand pleat. This will hold the box pleat in place.

PLEATED TABLECLOTH

Materials

Basic sewing kit (see page 176)
For a 29 in/72.5 cm high table, measuring 5 ft/1.5 m x 3 ft/1 m, you will need:
23 ft/7m fabric that is 54 in/135 cm wide
Glass-headed pins
6 frog fasteners

6 Lay the whole side panel on a flat surface right side up. Use pins to mark a point 2½ ft/0.75 m on either side of the central box pleat.

7 Fold each end of the panel into a box pleat; the pins mark the point of the first pleat fold. To do this, first make an 4 in/10 cm pleat, then fold another 4½ in/11.25 cm pleat underneath, to include a ½ in/1.25 cm seam allowance. Cut away any surplus fabric. Press.

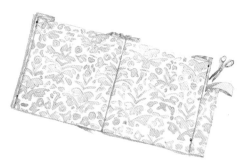

8 Repeat steps 4 to 7 to complete the skirt for the second long side of the table. Set aside. Measure up the fabric for the first short end of the skirt. Lay one of the end panels cut out in step 2 on a flat surface. Fold in half to find the middle. Mark a point 18 in/43 cm to either side of the central point with pins. The distance in between the pins measures the width of the tabletop.

9 Starting at the point marked by a pin, fold in a double pleat at either side of the panel. The top pleat should be 4 in/10cm wide and the underneath pleat 4½ in/11.25 cm wide, to include a ½ in/1.25 cm seam allowance. Trim off an excess ½ in/1.25 cm at each side. Press.

10 Lay the end panel over the side panel so that the pleats align and the ½ in/1.25 cm seam allowances overlap, right sides together. Pin and baste together and machine stitch.

11 As with the first box pleat made in step 5, fold back the pleat and machine down 3 in/7.5 cm from the top edge along the crease of the pleat to secure it. All four corners of the skirt are finished in this way. Repeat steps 8 to 11 until all four side panels are joined together to form the skirt.

Printed Fortuny fabric is used to make an elegant dining-room tablecloth with box pleats.

12 To attach the top of the cloth to the side panels: start at one corner. With the top panel right side down and the box pleated skirt wrong side out, pin and baste the two together, leaving a ½ in/1.25 cm seam allowance on both pieces. Machine together, working from one corner to another. Trim away any excess fabric and overlock the edges, see Techniques page 180.

13 To hem the skirt: turn in a 2½ in/7.25 cm fold all around the base of the skirt and press. Open out and fold in half again. Hand sew a double hem. Finally, hand sew the frog fasteners just below the surface of the table top across each of the six box pleats.

① Underneath a display of white ironstone pieces stands a high-backed bench and chairs which are upholstered in quilted matelasse cotton. The Orkney chair on the right is softened with a pillow. Light is filtered by woven shades or blinds and printed chintz drapes complete the window treatment.

② Unusually long ties on a pair of woven cotton seat squab are wound decoratively around the legs of two antique stripped wood chairs.

③④ In an east-facing breakfast room furnished with 18th-century painted pine panelling on the walls, a Shaker high chair and a plain candelabra, the central table is given a dual fabric treatment. The underlayer of heavy burlap or hessian is in keeping with the bare window and rougher textures.in the room such as the dark wicker chairs, while the overcloth of very fine white linen adds a note of sophistication.

③

Fabrics should be resistant to the onslaught of steam, heat and condensation that is generated as a result of cooking, washing and any amount of unavoidable splashes and spills, not to mention hectic family meals and more casual get-togethers. Here, tablecloths and covers can be less grand and elegant than in a separate and more formal dining area and it makes sense to opt for short, simple window treatments – these can be laundered much more easily than full-length dressings in order to remove food smells. Festoons and heavy valances or pelmets tend to be dust traps and are difficult to keep clean and the slats on Venetian shades or blinds also collect dirt and need regular cleaning. In a well-used kitchen area drapes should stop just above the sill and never be allowed to trail over the sink or flap near the stove. Instead, wipe-clean roller shades or blinds with a plasticized or other washable surface are a sensible choice.

④

SUNFLOWER APPLIQUE CHAIR COVER

Materials

Basic sewing kit (see page 176)
Approximately 2 yd 7 in/2 m main fabric per chair
Contrasting fabric for piping and appliqué motif
Piping cord
Iron-on adhesive webbing or fabric stiffener

1 Measure the chair back from the top to the floor (A) and the width of the back (B); add ½ in/1.25 cm seam allowance all around. Cut out a panel of main fabric.

2 Measure the front of the chair down the inside back and across the depth of the seat and add an all-around ½ in/1.25 cm seam allowance. Cut out a panel of main fabric.

3 Measure the length and width of the sides and the front of the chair below seat level. Measure from the seat to the floor for the length (C) and from outside edge of chair leg to outside edge of chair leg for the width (D). Add an all-around ½ in/1.25 cm seam allowance. Cut out three panels of main fabric.

4 Make enough corded piping to edge the panel made in step 2 and the entire skirt of the chair, see Techniques page 181 .

5 Iron the contrasting appliqué fabric onto adhesive webbing or fabric stiffener. Cut out a sunflower shape.

6 Pin the appliqué sunflower to the middle of the right side of the back panel and hand sew in position.

7 Turn in the seam allowance all around the front panel made in step 2 and press. Pin and baste the piping closely all around the folded edge, tucking the open edges of the piping inward against the seam allowance of the panel. Hand sew the piping in place.

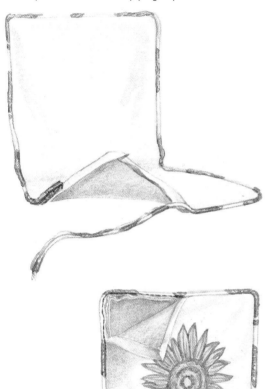

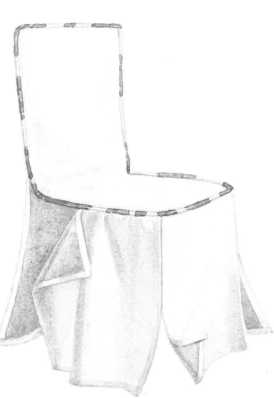

Yellow and white cottons and linens complement wicker chairs. A wooden chair is transformed with an elegant white linen loose cover with a sunflower appliquéd on the back.

9 Pin and baste the two side panels to the front panel of the skirt, right sides together. Machine stitch halfway down the join, leaving an opening to trim the corners with piping. Press. To join the skirt to the main front panel of the chair, pin and baste the two panels right sides together, aligning the folds of the two seam allowances. Machine stitch together a fraction outside the line of machine stitching on the piping. Turn right side out and press.

10 Hand sew more piping around the perimeter of the two side panels and the front and back skirts. Finish any ends with neat hand stitches to prevent fraying. Trim all excess seam allowances on the reverse side of the loose cover. Press the whole and slip over the chair.

8 Place the back panel and the front panel right sides together. Pin and baste. Machine stitch the two together to the point where the back of the chair meets the seat and turn right side out. Press.

①

②

③

④

⑤

However, fabrics are used for many other purposes in the dining room or kitchen apart from dressing windows and tables. They help to provide textural contrast in an area that is full of unyielding surfaces and they can often add much-needed accent colors in order to contrast or co-ordinate with the theme of the room. Well-chosen touches can help to enliven a bland, neutral look, brighten a dull scheme or calm down an over-busy one, warm up a cool interior or cool down rather "hot" shades. When it comes to choosing color schemes for this part of the house there are several points to consider in addition to the usual factors such as the basic size, shape and outlook of the room as well as the amount of daylight that the interior receives.

If you are planning a dining room or kitchen from scratch choose the ingredients with care as they are likely to be with you for a long time. Built-in cabinets or units, work counters or free-standing pieces of furniture such as servers or dressers will dominate. Similarly, dark furniture may be oppressive when installed wall-to-wall and cluttered shelves or sideboards can soon tire the eyes. Use fabrics to relieve and lighten or complement the existing furniture.

A shared kitchen and dining area is likely to be warm from the heat generated by cooking and other domestic chores, so it is a good place to use cool shades such as blue, green or lilac on the main surfaces and perhaps a warmer shade added on smaller areas for contrast. If the space is small and you want to make it appear larger, as well as choosing a cool, receding scheme, select soft furnishings with a similar tonal value and use the same color for the floor, walls and window treatments – so that the window does not break up the wall area. This "all-of-a-piece" treatment will enlarge the space visually. To avoid too much uniformity include some

contrasting textures. If you wish to create the opposite effect and make a large room appear smaller and more intimate then use a darker or warmer advancing main color and introduce contrast in the form of an eye-catching design on the floor, stencils on the walls or patterned window dressings and accessories.

Here, as in any other part of the house, the overall impression will be achieved through a combination of color, pattern, texture and form. Whatever style you eventually choose, you may find it a help to have a starting point: an

(8)

(6)

(7)

(1) In an old farmhouse, the rustic wooden dining table is covered with an antique lace-edged cloth.

(2) Hard-wearing printed cotton is used to line the shelves and interior of a display cabinet. The patterned fabric beautifully sets off a collection of antique glass and porcelain.

(3) Large, comfortable wing chairs loose-covered in creamy linen are arranged around a heavy sawbuck table to make for relaxing mealtimes.

(4) Woven linen in a rich forest green enhances a dining-room chair. The drapes behind are in a comple-mentary green jacquard weave.

(5) Wool tartan drapes hang from a wrought-iron rod at the window of a country dining room. The Windsor chairs at the table have matching tartan seat squabs.

(6) A simple country table setting includes a pressed patterned glass, an earthenware jug and a woven napkin bunched inside a ring of woven twigs.

(7) Checked cotton makes a delightful accompaniment to food. Here assorted napkins have pretty frayed edges.

(8) Numerous cotton napkins and glasscloths or tea towels hang beneath a kitchen mantel shelf that is laden with china in a celebration of blue and white.

(1)

(1) The dual use of fabrics creates an attractive table treatment. A delicate lace-edged undercloth works as a deep frill and is protected by a more practical cotton gingham overcloth.

(2) Cream linen drapes in a bay window are topped with an antique *toile de Jouy* valance or pelmet with a scalloped edge. The window treatment ties in with the large-check woven linen cloth on the table.

(3) Arched French windows leading off an octagonal breakfast alcove are treated with simple beige linen drapes tied to rings along a wooden pole.

interesting accessory, a set of cooking utensils, a particular piece of fabric – any of these may suggest a theme. For example, you may wish to create a monochromatic contemporary setting with a predominance of black, white and gray and add glossy cabinets or fitted kitchen units, a studded rubber floor, industrial shelving, plenty of stainless steel and some commercial catering implements on view, a chrome serving trolley and micro shades or blinds at the window. Then you can add color accents and soften the hard lines with other accessories. For a Scandinavian-style setting choose well-designed cabinets or units made from a combination of sleek laminate and warm wood; opt for a blue and yellow scheme with color-washed tongue-and-groove boards on the walls and introduce subtle checks and stripes at the windows and in other fabric details. You can evoke a Mediterranean flavor with earthenware floor tiles, roughly plastered walls, stippled or distressed wood furniture and add color accents in the form of herb-filled terra-cotta pots.

Keep the window treatments simple – wooden internal shutters are appropriate, or try a basic Holland shade or blind or a soft length of muslin or calico or any other open-weave light-filtering fabric draped over a simple pole or rod; other suitable fabrics include bleached canvas, natural linen or checked seersucker.

For those who prefer a country-style ambience, the unfitted or free-standing kitchen is appropriate and individual pieces of furniture, perhaps in a variety of woods, can be set off with natural textures and neutral or fresh pastel colors. Painted or distressed wood can look spectacular in a kitchen and you can pull the various elements in the scheme together in a variety of ways. For instance, kitchen chairs can be made more comfortable and co-ordinated

with the theme with the addition of tie-on squab cushions for both the back and the seat; as an alternative, tie-on or slip-on covers can even engulf the whole chair in a pretty, washable wrapping. Another idea is to use pleated fabric behind glazed or chicken-wire covered cabinet doors; fix the cloth by threading it along a wire with eyelets in the fabric, or use tacks. You can also line drawers, or drop-in cutlery trays or baskets with fabric – this is both attractive and practical as the lining can be removed and laundered to prevent a build-up of dust.

There is a plethora of fabric accessories for the kitchen and adjoining utility room. Aprons, oven gloves, tea and coffee pot cosies, egg cosies, napkins, bread roll holders, peg bags, laundry baskets, ironing board covers and much more can be chosen to co-ordinate with china, pottery, glassware, trays, chopping boards, storage containers and boxes and many other items. They may be selected to blend in to a specific color scheme or chosen on more of an ad-hoc mix and match basis to provide colorful and textural contrast.

(3)

④⑤ A high-ceilinged dining room accomodates four separate tables. These are covered in a variety of cloths made of rough beige linen and red linen gingham. In the forground, the tabletop consists of a square of raffia bordered with linen. The detail shows co-ordinating linen napkins rolled up in raffia rings.

⑥ Large pillows or cushions covered in printed linen fill a deep window seat in a country kitchen. Tailored cotton loose covers on a set of antique chairs look fresh and inviting.

⑦ A strong gingham check tablecloth dominates chairs covered in linen *toile de Jouy*. The striped cotton drapes match the fabric that is used to line and screen the doors of a large cupboard.

④

⑤

⑥

⑦

1 Measure the table top and add an allowance for the drop on all four sides. You will need to make four lengths of scallop border to attach to the main cloth. Calculate the scallop size so that each corner ends on a half scallop which will be mitered to another half scallop.

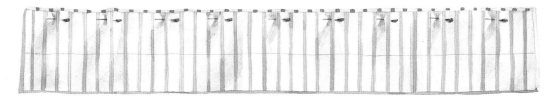

2 To make one side of the scallop border; place two lengths of the contrasting fabric right sides together. Pin along the top edge. Make sure that the pattern aligns on both sides. Draw a straight line across the middle of the fabric with a long metal ruler and a marker pen. Repeat for the three remaining sides of the border.

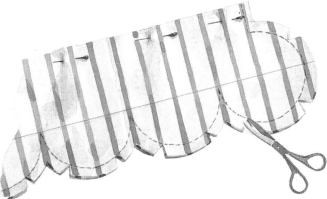

3 Using a round template, such as a plate, mark the outline of the scallops the length of one side of the border with a marker pen, ending on a three-quarter scallop. This outline will be the stitching line.

4 Cut out the scallops ½ in/1.5 cm outside the trace line. Make snips at intervals along the curved edges so that the fabric lies flat. Secure with pins and machine along the trace line.

An antique linen sheet with a monogram is turned into an elegant tablecloth and trimmed with a scallop border in striped cotton.

5 Turn the scallop border right side out and iron flat. Repeat for the three remaining sides of the border.

6 To join the four sides of the border: miter the corners by overlapping two ¾ scallops. Tuck the excess ¼ scallop inside the end scallop so that it is not visible. Make sure that the pattern aligns and hand sew the straight edges together in a neat miter, see Techniques, page 180. Press.

SCALLOP BORDER TABLECLOTH
Materials

Basic sewing kit (see page 176)
Main fabric for tablecloth
Contrasting fabric for scallop border
Template for scallops such as a glass, cup or plate
Long metal ruler   Marker pen

7 Cut the main fabric ½ in/1.5 cm larger all around than the area inside the scallop border. Slip this layer of fabric in between the two open layers that form the inside edge of the border. Turn under the straight edge of the border and pin and baste to the main cloth around all four sides. Turn the whole over and repeat on the reverse side. Press. Hand sew the main fabric and the scallop border together on both sides of the tablecloth.

BEDROOMS are usually situated away from the commotion of family and domestic life and consequently they can be decorated with a little more indulgence and a little less consideration to practicality than other rooms of the house. Here in particular, fragile fabrics, pale colors and opulent textures can come into their own. For many of us the bedroom is much more than a place to sleep, for it is also a peaceful and private retreat. And because it is such a highly personal space it should ideally be decorated to suit the needs and reflect the personality of its main occupant or occupants.

Some bedrooms are connected to a dressing area or a bathroom. If this is the case, you can link the scheme visually between one area and another to create a sense of space and continuity. It helps to use the same flooring throughout and perhaps soften it with matching bathroom and bedside rugs. You might choose a co-ordinating fabric for the bedding and echo the pattern on the drapes or curtains at the bedroom window and on a shade or blind in the bathroom. Or paper the bedroom walls in a suitable pattern and then add a matching frieze to plain bathroom walls.

The bedroom is primarily a place for sleep, rest and relaxation so the scheme should not be too stimulating. Avoid very bold colors, strong patterns and too many shiny textures and opt instead for a harmonious scheme using colors that are close to each other in the color wheel. For example, use blues, greens and lavenders or lilacs with sparkling white for a cool and elegant effect; apricots, yellows, greens or blues for a sunny Mediterranean look and pinks or peaches with cream for a warmer, more intimate ambience. You may wish to achieve a blend-and-tone effect with a monochromatic scheme based on different strengths or tones of one color. However, take note that very dark colors absorb light and certain tones, in particular the yellowy-greens, can look gloomy at night unless they are well lit. In general, most bedrooms benefit from subtle and restrained background lighting with a few additional task lights for bedside reading and at the dressing table.

When choosing the color scheme make use of paint manufacturers' swatches as a helpful reference. Once you have decided on your main color the conventional treatment is to take a deep value for the floor, a mid-tone for the walls, a shade or two paler for the ceiling and the lightest value for any woodwork.

Bedrooms

Opposite A magnificent early 18th-century American four-poster bed is simply adorned with a canopy of handkerchief linen.

(1) A detail of the bed hangings on an oak-framed bed. The inside of the drapes are trimmed with fine hem-stitched linen which is buttoned to the main burlap or hessian with antique bone buttons and can be detached for cleaning.

(2) Rough burlap or hessian drapes hung from a chunky oak frame draw to enclose the bed.

(3) The only pattern present in this bedroom is the strong brown and cream squares painted on the walls to simulate fresco plaster. This provides a backdrop to the bed – dressed with crisp, white handkerchief linens – and the side table which is covered in a simple hem-stitched fine linen and set off with an 18th-century tole candlestick.

(4) Country cotton plaid tied to a rough twig pole fixed to the wall on a pair of brackets makes a simple bed hanging. A blue and white Indian cotton tablecloth acts as a summer bedspread in this spare loft or attic bedroom.

You can integrate the basic color scheme with a patterned fabric for the window and bed treatments which incorporates all the selected monochromatic tones, or you can introduce a color contrast – which may be warm, cool or neutral depending on the main color theme; finally echo the contrast in accessories.

A neutral scheme is the ideal way to create a relaxing atmosphere in any room. For a really light bedroom try cool white walls, woodwork and ceiling and a heavily textured, quilted, piqué or matelasse bedcover in off-white. At the windows you could use drapes over rattan shades or blinds, while the floor might be a natural sisal or rush matting. You could complete the scheme with limed woodwork and furniture and a touch of fresh green, for accents.

In a large room the bed can be treated so that it is the focus of attention. The overall impact will depend to some extent on the way that you choose to drape and dress the bed, but your choice of color and pattern is also

④

important. To define the bed you should color it to contrast with its surroundings; for instance, pick a bold pattern for the bedcovers and any overhead treatments and team this with plain walls and floor. Or you may wish to reverse this approach and use a strong, plain color for the bed and perhaps pipe or trim it to add contrast and outline the shape against softly patterned walls and a strongly textured carpet. In a small bedroom, in order to create an impression of space, limit the number of colors used in the scheme and instead provide visual interest with textural contrast so that the room does not appear too uniform.

When decorating the bedroom do not discount the ceiling, as along with the bathroom this is a room where it will not pass unnoticed. If you want to make the ceiling appear higher, instead of just painting it white be more imaginative and color it a value or two lighter than the walls or paint it to match the background to your chosen wallcovering. If you are using a small, neat geometric or mini-print paper or fabric on the walls then you can continue this over the ceiling – this looks particularly effective in a loft or attic or dormer situation where there is a sloping ceiling – so long as the pattern is non-directional, otherwise accurate pattern-matching will be extremely difficult. Avoid using borders and other embellishments in this type of interior, unless you expressly wish to outline the interesting shapes that are created by the slope.

The advantage of tenting fabric is that it need not be expensive and unlike fabric for drapes and curtains it does not have to be sun- and fade-resistant so you can consider using a dressmaking fabric. Lining for drapes and curtains is available in all sorts of colors other than traditional cream.

The same method is used for making the top canopy and all the side drapes. The top canopy is attached to the frame with ties; the drapes are suspended by loops.

1 For the top canopy, measure the length and width of the bed and add a 1½ in/4.5 cm seam allowance all around. Cut out a panel of each main fabric. If necessary, seam together widths to make the panel wide enough.

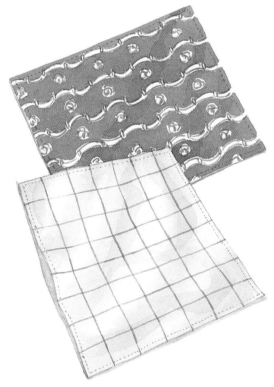

Large cotton checks combined with a cotton floral print frame a bed which dominates a small bedroom.

2 For each of the six drapes and the back drape, measure the frame of the bed and include a 1½ in/4.5 cm seam allowance at the top and sides. Cut out the required length and width in each main fabric.

3 To make the first drape, take the contrasting fabric and cut out enough 2 in/5 cm wide strips on the bias to go around all four sides of the floral fabric panel. Fold the strips in half lengthways and iron down, right side out. This will form the contrast edging.

4 To make the loops for the first drape, take the contrasting fabric and cut out five strips 8 in/20 cm long and 1½ in/4.5 cm wide. Turn in ¼ in/0.75 cm down each long edge and press. Fold in half lengthways, wrong sides together, and press again. Machine stitch the long folded edges together.

(The same method applies for making the 16 ties used to attach the top canopy to the bed frame. Cut out each tie 28 in/70 cm long and 1½ in/3.75 cm wide. To finish the open edge of each tie, make a small double fold and hand stitch neatly.)

5 Place the main fabric panel right side up and lay the contrast edging along the outside edge of the panel with folded edge facing out. Pin and baste in place. (The illustration below shows the top canopy. Place two ties at each end of the short edge and space the rest evenly in between them and down each side.) Fold the ties in half around the band of contrast edging, as shown in the detail below right. Pin and baste in place.
For the side drapes and back drape, attach the loops along the top edge only, as shown below left.

FOUR-POSTER BED HANGINGS
Materials

Basic sewing kit (see page 176)
Floral fabric to make six side drapes,
one back drape and a top canopy
Check fabric to make six drapes,
one back drape and a top canopy
About 5 ½ yd/5 m fabric for
contrast edging and loops and ties

6 Place the second panel of main fabric onto the first panel, right sides facing. Pin and baste together around all four sides, taking in the contrast edging. Machine stitch, leaving an opening on one side to turn the whole right side out. The ties (or loops) should appear in between the two panels of main fabric. Turn right side out. Press.

7 Tie the top canopy to the top of the bed frame with the ties. Hang the side drapes and back drape from the bed rail with the loops, by dismantling the top of the bed frame.

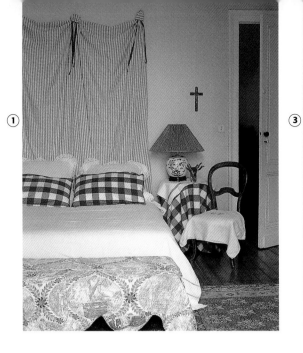

① A panel of striped cotton is bunched over wall-mounted bosses and tied with a ribbon to form an attractive backdrop to a bed. The stool in the foreground is draped with antique *toile de Jouy*.

② A large bedroom window is dressed with a double pair of unlined printed cotton drapes in contrasting patterns. In the foreground, a cotton and lace bedspread lies on a plump feather bed.

③ Purple cotton gingham is used to upholster the base of a bed to make it an attractive feature of the whole construction. Above the bed a canopy of fine white butter muslin hangs from a wooden coronet.

(4)

(4) A bedroom chair loose-covered in beige cotton ticking; the fabric is fastened to the seat with contrasting ties made of cheerful red binding tape.

(5) Pieces of antique linen are now collectable items. Here, a well-preserved linen glasscloth or tea towel serves as a crisp bedside tablecloth.

(6) In a bedroom corner, an ordinary checked cotton undercloth is overlaid with an antique embroidered lace-edged bed sheet from Sweden.

(7) Situated by a window to take advantage of the light, a draped table is paired with a comfortable armchair with a beige cotton ticking loose cover.

(6)

Lining has an attractive sheen which helps to reflect light. Sheeting is a suitable alternative for tenting and as it is extra-wide it is economical. Sheeting is available in a wide choice of pastel shades and stronger colors, as well as some florals, polka dots, random spots and mini-print geometrics. For a totally co-ordinated look you can tent the ceiling to match the bedding.

If tenting is too dramatic a treatment for your taste, then there are various ways of draping the bed itself in order to achieve an opulent look. While many of us might dream of a magnificent four-poster with carved posts and sumptuous drapes rising to lambrequined canopies; most bedrooms today are neither tall enough nor spacious enough to accommodate such a top-heavy structure, never mind the budget needed for such a bed! However, it is possible to simulate a four-poster with a simple frame consisting of slender posts which can be attached to the base of the bed at each corner. You can also use fabric without the need for corner posts because drapes or hangings can be suspended from a ceiling-mounted track or pole which must be carefully positioned to align with the size and shape of the bed below – this arrangement requires meticulous measuring and you will need to draw a ceiling as well as a floor plan to scale in order to plot the position of the track or pole exactly.

You can also create an effective half-tester with a valance and a wall- or ceiling-mounted double track, similar to the type used for mounting drapes or curtains at the window. The valance or pelmet serves to conceal the workings of the drapes. An alternative way of hanging drapes for either treatment is to use ceiling-mounted poles – with one attached parallel to the foot of the bed and the other parallel to the head. With a single bed two

(5)

(7)

shorter poles can be attached parallel to each side of the bed, to stop about halfway down the length of the bed and then drapes or "falls" of fabric can be thrown over the pole to simulate the traditional bed drapes of the four-poster.

A cozy alternative which works well in a small room with a single bed and an idea which is particularly popular with children involves creating a bed-in-a-closet. Build wardrobes the same depth as the width of the bed, along one wall of the room, then link the two sets of wardrobes with smaller closets along the top which will leave an alcove for the bed. Fix drapes or curtains from a track underneath the small closets situated over the alcove and conceal the track behind a batten, valance or pelmet. These drapes can then be drawn to enclose the bed, so giving total privacy at night. This idea can also be adapted to box in a bath and, particularly if it is combined with a shower, the curtains should be fully waterproof. For more ideas on fabric canopies over a bathtub, see the chapter on Bathrooms, pages 130-7.

① In a loft or attic bedroom a tent-like bed is constructed using lengths of cream cotton which are slung over hooks in the ceiling. The bed itself is swathed in luxurious crumpled antique linen sheets.

② A detail of the bed linen in the same room shows beautiful drawn threadwork and embroidered initials.

③ Gauze-like cotton voile is draped generously at the windows and around the four-poster bed in a cool blend of ice-blue and white; a suitable color scheme for a bedroom in a warm climate. The checked cotton bed blanket provides a subtle splash of pattern.

There are various ways of creating sumptuous over-bed drapes. These work especially well in rooms where there is one long, unbroken wall against which the bed can be positioned – either with the length parallel to the wall or with the head of the bed set against the wall. If the room is square or generally lacking in interest then the contrast of form created by an over-bed drape can provide a dramatic focal point. Decorating periods of the past are a rich and varied source of inspiration for decorative hangings. For example, the Empire-style bed traditionally had a curved head- and footboard and was placed lengthways against a wall. A swathe of cloth was slung over a pole or suspended from a corona fixed high up on the wall above and the fabric then fell freely over the head- and foot boards to frame the bed. In some cases the flowing fabric can also be caught and held in position with bosses fixed to the wall in line with each end of the bed. Today, such ideas can be interpreted more simply: try attaching a single pole above the bed with fabric draped over it or slot-headed onto the pole and then catch the fabric back on either side of the bedhead. Coronas are another, more luxurious way of suspending fabric above the bed. These are usually wall- or ceiling-mounted and have a semi-circular or coronet-shaped frame which hides a track supporting the drape – the fabric can also be stapled or pinned to the frame.

Whatever type of ceiling tenting or over-bed drapes you choose they tend to be dust traps and will require cleaning. Regular vacuuming will help and paler colors can be treated for stain- and dirt-resistance. However, eventually dry cleaning or laundering will be necessary and occasionally the hanging will have to be taken down, so take this into consideration when deciding on the method of fixing.

④ Beds can be scattered with pillows or cushions for comfort and decoration. A bolster and a plump pair of striped silk taffeta pillows with ruffled edges sit on fine Egyptian cotton sheets.

⑤ A French *fauteuil* chair with an oval back has been loose-covered with cream cotton and the skirt has been prettily gathered and piped.

⑥ Bare painted floorboards and stark, high-backed metal chairs contrast well with the luxurious comfort of a Polonaise-style canopied bed dressed with quantities of printed silk taffeta. The head- and footboard are upholstered in matching fabric.

⑦ Tasselled tie-backs in complementary colors hold back the cascading draperies above the bed.

(1) To block out the bustle of an urban environment, a town-house bedroom is insulated with fabric-covered wall panels. To increase the cocoon effect, lined and interlined wool drapes with thick wool carpeting provide an abundance of warm textures. The bed is an expanse of white cotton broken by a pair of throw pillows with a contrasting hand-stitched pattern.

(2) Floor-to-ceiling beige wool drapes with a neat smocked heading surround a double bed and add warmth to the room. The headboard is upholstered in fine wool to complement the wall treatment.

(3) For a contemporary look, built-in wood bedside tables and plain walls are coupled with plain white linens.

(4) The dust ruffle or valance on the bed in the same room is made from fine Egyptian cotton. There is a double kick pleat at the corner and the hem is embroidered with a triple row of black overlocking.

(5) To echo the detail on the dust ruffle or valance the white pillowcases on the same bed are edged with a triple row of black stitching. The headboard behind is upholstered in white cotton poplin and trimmed with two rows of piping and large, covered buttons.

112

However stylishly "dressed" a bed may look, it must also be comfortable to lie on or sleep in. The choice of bedding is a matter of personal taste, but easy care is of prime importance. Fabrics which need frequent laundering, such as sheets, pillowcases and quilt covers, should be able to withstand regular washing and any textile chosen to cover a bed should be color-fast and shrink-resistant and specifically designed for the purpose – this is not a good place to use dressmaking fabrics.

Dust ruffles or valances which skirt the base of the bed are useful for disguising unsightly bed bases or to conceal storage space in between the mattress and the floor. Because these do not need to be changed for washing as frequently as other bedding they can be made in a heavier fabric and you may wish to co-ordinate or contrast them with the drapes or curtains in the room or the bedcover itself. Box-pleated dust ruffles or valances are elegant and can be trimmed or piped to define the pleats – you will need to use a firm fabric such as cotton sateen, chintz, ticking, closely woven cotton, linen or a linen and cotton mix.

Quilts and covers should be selected to suit the style of the room as well as the size and shape of the bed. In some cases the duvet with its own cover is left on view as part of the scheme, but you may prefer to supplement this with a bedcover. Where a bed has posts or head- and footboards, a throw-over or tailored cover may be suitable or you could use a shorter cover to come part-way down to hide the mattress and combine this with a dust ruffle or valance to conceal the base of the bed. There are also luxurious throw-overs which combine duvet and bedcover in one: the top is quilted and fabric flows freely to the floor on either side of the bed while the edge is finished with a rich trimming

(1)

(3)

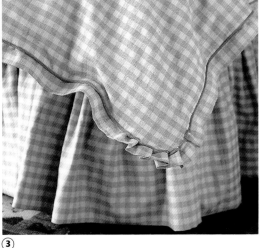

(4)

(2)

or neat piping. A layered look is also popular for beds, for instance, comforters, patchwork quilts or fleecy blankets may be combined with a crochet or lace top-cover, throws and shawls and then accessorized with numerous pillows or cushions and plump bolsters. This kind of treatment will give the bed greater impact in the room. Whatever type of quilt or bed covering you choose, you should always consider the practicalities of cleaning and laundering.

For smaller rooms simpler treatments may be the sensible option. To simulate a couch for a dual-purpose bedroom or for a young person's bed-sitting room take a neat, tailored cover with matching full-width bolsters at the head and foot of a single bed placed lengthways against the wall, then finish the effect with an assortment of pillows or cushions propped in between the bolsters along the wall. In some situations the head of the bed may require an attached headboard. Head- and footboards are available in all sort of materials and a variety of forms. Fabric-covered headboards are comfortable to lean against and can be designed to match other soft furnishings in the room for an integrated scheme. You might choose a stripe, check, geometric pattern or a plain fabric to link with the rest of the scheme and add piping to outline

(5)

(1)(2) A fully upholstered bed dressed in white linen. The footboard retains its clean outline because the well-tailored loose cover forms a perfect fit.

(3) The pleated rounded corner of a quilt cover made from a cotton check shown in detail. Underneath is a gathered dust ruffle or valance in matching fabric.

(4) On the same bed, a padded headboard continues the check theme and scatter pillows with double gathered ruffled edges complete the all-in-one look.

(5) Starfish and seashells are embroidered onto bed linen for a seaside theme in a beach-house bedroom.

(6) Against a buttoned headboard covered in plain linen floral linen pillows are finished with a mattress-like edging. A cotton honeycomb blanket lies on the bed.

(7) Linen, a versatile and hard-wearing furnishing fabric is used here to tight-cover a bedroom chair. The plain beige is spiced up with a striped linen pillow.

(8) Beige and white linen abounds in a smart bedroom. The walls are upholstered in fine pin-stripe linen and the fully lined and interlined linen drapes have elegant pinch pleat headings.

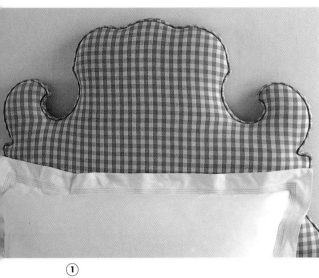

①

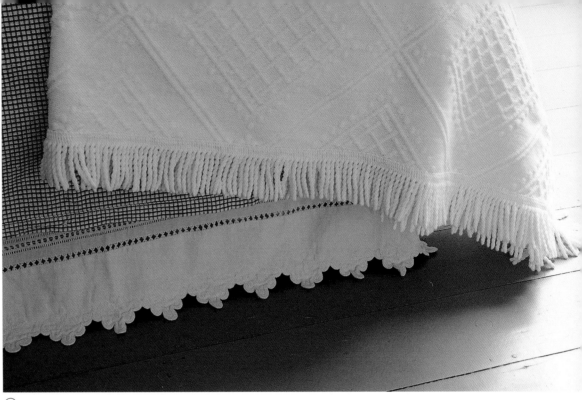

③

②

④

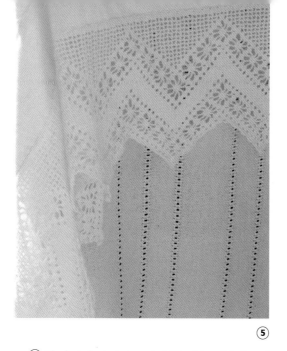

(1) Headboards lend themsleves to all kinds of fabric treatments; you can loose-cover or upholster them to contrast or co-ordinate with the overall scheme of a bedroom. Here, an elaborately shaped headboard has been well padded for comfort and then tight-covered with checked cotton. The unusual outline is defined with an edge of self-piping. Underneath, a pillow is cased in fine cotton.

(2) A woven rattan bed frame is dressed with fresh cotton sheets and a woven cotton blanket. The window treatment in the background consists of richly gathered muslin drapes which hang over painted bamboo shutters that are screened with tied-on panels of raffia.

(5)

(3) The foot of a bed, shown in full in picture 4, is draped with a heavy, fringed cotton bedspread. This detail shows how an antique lace cotton sheet has been adapted to form a pretty dust ruffle or valance.

(4) A loft bedroom is light and airy with a combination of pristine white cotton and country checks. The bed linen echoes the ingenious round window treatment.

(5) A delicate antique lace-edged cotton cloth is combined with a drawn threadwork panel.

(6) A variety of textured white cottons on a bed.

the shape. Separate headboards can be mounted on the wall or else you can wall-mount a pole or a rod, positioned at a suitable height above the bed, and suspend flat squab cushions from it by means of ties or loops for an inexpensive and stylish look. To work out the size, shape and effect of any bedhead or over-bed treatment you should initially make an elevation or scale drawing in plan of the wall and then test for effect using various shapes drawn on an overlay, as suggested for window treatments. To test the overall effect of bed hangings you can use old sheeting as a guide and attach it to the wall behind or above the bed.

Whatever textiles you select for any of the bedhead ideas that are suggested here they will need to be easy to clean, so consider the benefits of loose or slip covers and use shrink- and fade-proof fabric with rust-proof and color-fast fixings and trimmings to prevent damage during cleaning. It is also sensible to treat a fixed headboard cover so that it is stain-resistant.

Other items of bedroom furniture can be given various softening touches; for example, wardrobes or closets with glazed doors look much prettier with a pleated fabric fixed behind the glass to hide the contents from view. To achieve this, thread the panel of pleated fabric onto a wire through a system of eyelets or else simply tack the cloth to the inside of the door frame. Bedside tables can be smartened up with a "skirted" treatment or else given a layered look, perhaps with a floor-length patterned fabric cover overlaid with a shorter plain, square cloth and finished with lace, antique crochet or another open-weave top layer. Similarly you can embellish a dressing table with a double layer of skirted fabric such as spotted voile, muslin, organza or another sheer fabric perhaps placed over a plain, richly colored chintz.

1 Measure the dimensions of the bedhead and add a
¾ in/2 cm seam allowance around the top and
sides and a 1½ in/4 cm seam allowance
along the bottom. Cut out two
pieces of main fabric.

2 For the gusset: measure the perimeter and depth of
the bedhead and add ¾ in/2 cm seam allowance all
around. Cut out a strip of main fabric on the bias (join
strips together if necessary), see Techniques page 181.

3 Make up enough corded
piping to measure twice the perimeter
of the bed head, see Techniques page 181.

4 Iron a piece of contrasting fabric onto
adhesive webbing or fabric stiffener and cut out the
required shape, in this case a star.

LOOSE COVER FOR BEDHEAD

Materials

Basic sewing kit (see page 176)
Bed head
Main fabric
Contrasting fabric for appliqué
Adhesive webbing or iron-on fabric stiffener
Piping cord

5 Overlock the appliqué shape onto the right side of one of the main fabric panels made in step 1, see Techniques page 180. (Position the motif in the middle of the fabric.)

6 Pin and baste or tack the front panel to the gusset made in step 2, inserting the piping made in step 3 in between. Machine stitch right sides together. Repeat to join the back panel to the gusset, again inserting the second length of piping in between. Turn right side out.

7 Fold up ½ in/1.25 cm at the bottom of the main panels. Pin and baste. Hem by hand, see Techniques page 178. Press and pull down over the bedhead.

In a 19th-century cottage bedroom a simple Gothic-style bedhead is covered in hard-wearing cotton poplin and livened up with a large appliqué star.

(1) Pink cotton ticking on a shaped headboard is edged with contrast piping to highlight the outline.

(2) When covering head- or footboards on a bed with fabric, it is important to keep the grain straight so that any pattern is not distorted. Here the large checks are perfectly square.

(3) You can personalize plain pillowcases and sheets with decorative stitching. In this room, the bed linen is beautifully cross-stitched in a traditional East European pattern. A homespun lavender pillow with a red cross-stitched heart is a perfect gift idea.

(4) A linen pillowcase with delicate drawn threadwork contrasts with a red gingham cotton sheet.

(5) Machine-embroidered sheets and a pillowcase are finished with an appliquéd blue edging and coupled with an antique quilt.

(6) Clever color scheming of red, white and blue patterned cottons creates a harmonious effect. The dust ruffle or valance corresponds with the Roman shade or blind; the skirted chair is echoed in the floor rug; and the pillow and the narrow drapes held back with a simple metal hook echo the quilted bedspread.

④

⑤

⑥

①

②

③

④

⑤

If there is sufficient space, you may wish to create a small area in the bedroom where you can sit and relax – perhaps two easy elbow- or armchairs placed around a small table in a bay window, a *chaise longue* positioned parallel to the foot of a double bed and smothered in sumptuous pillows or cushions or an ottoman at the foot of a single bed.

A window seat is a practical alternative when space is short. Both an ottoman and a window seat would make useful storage space for spare bedding as well as a place to sit. Add a lift-up, padded top and plenty of plump pillows or cushions for a softening effect. The fabric can match, co-ordinate or contrast with the drapes or curtains or the window seat may be part of a mix-and-match scheme. For imaginative ideas on how to use fabric for pretty and personal finishing touches in the bedroom, in particular how to style the interior with a range of pillows or cushions and decorative lampshades, see the chapter on Accessories, pages 148-73.

If there is a shortage of storage space in the bedroom then you can make use of existing alcoves which may be situated on either side of a chimney breast. Alcoves are often left unused, but you can install shelves and then cover the gap with a drape or curtain or a shade or blind to hide the shelves from view. To dress up a fairly narrow alcove you can attach a cornice or pelmet or a batten across the top in order to hang a roller shade or blind below. Note that roll-down shades or blinds only operate efficiently if the span is not too wide as the roller and slat-lifting mechanism can only take a certain amount of strain; manufacturers give recommended maximum widths in their measuring-up instructions. As an alternative, a fabric-covered folding screen can be an attractive way to cover shelves or alcoves.

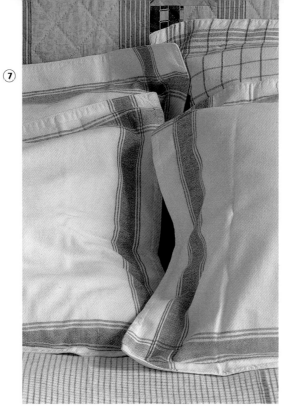

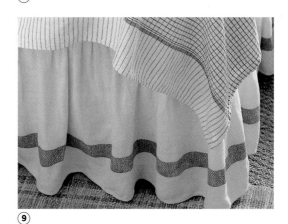

1. A richly colored quilt, is given a new lease of life with a hand-sewn border of taffeta plaid ribbon.

2. Matelasse is a heavy, quilted fabric; edged in red plaid it hangs well as a bedside tablecloth.

3. To blend with a bold patchwork bedspread (see picture 5), cotton batik is draped over the side table and a heavy cotton throw covers the floor.

4. An old blue and white homespun pillowcase retains its original white cotton ties.

5. An assortment of old glasscloths or tea towels have been converted into an original patchwork bedspread. The cloths were cut into squares of equal size and the edges frayed by pulling a few threads along the sides.

6. At one end of a panelled bedroom, a large dressing table is draped in an antique damask cloth.

7. Bed linen woven to resemble traditional cotton glasscloths or tea towels strikes a crisp, fresh note.

8. Real glasscloths or tea towels are used for this lined and edged bedspread. The gathered dust ruffle or valance is made from a candystripe cotton.

9. A woven bedspread complements the fine soft cotton that skirts the base of a bed.

10. In a farmhouse bedroom a beautiful old quilt hangs on the wall at the head of a king-size bed.

1 Cut all the hems off the glasscloths or tea towels. Lay out in the pattern shown opposite.

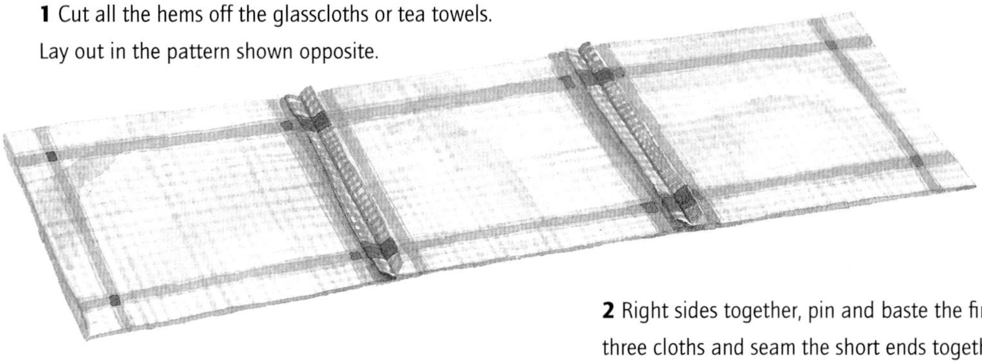

2 Right sides together, pin and baste the first three cloths and seam the short ends together; make sure that the checks align.

3 Repeat for the next four strips. Seam all five strips together along each long edge and iron flat.

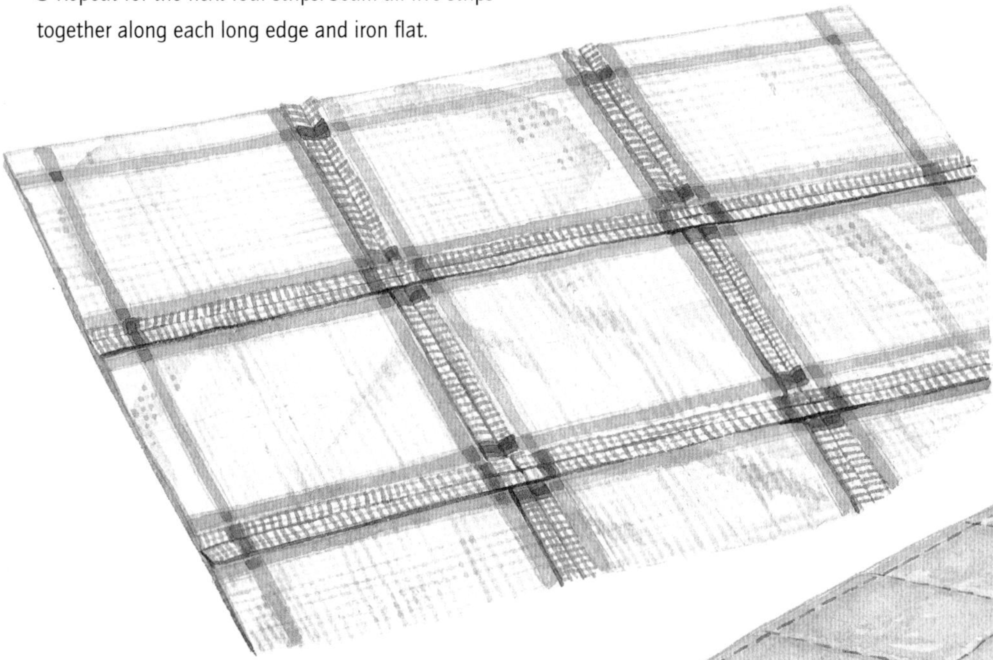

4 Lay the interlining fabric on a flat surface and cut out to the required overall size of the bedspread. If you need to join widths of fabric to achieve the required size, overlap widths by ½ in/1.25 cm and use a zigzag stitch to achieve a flat seam.

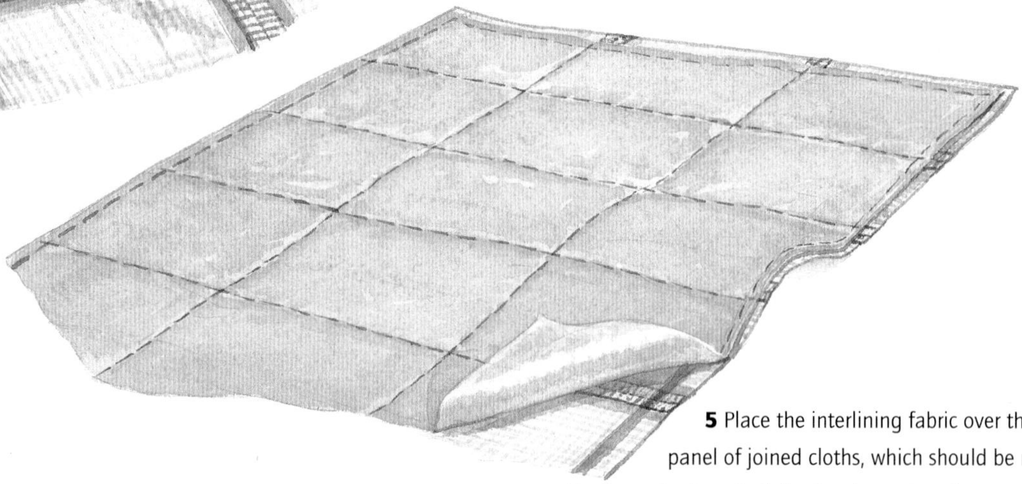

5 Place the interlining fabric over the panel of joined cloths, which should be right side down. Baste or tack the two layers together, following the outline of each glasscloth or tea towel, then baste all around the perimeter.

Kitchen glasscloths or tea towels make a smart bedspread in a bedroom full of country gingham checks and stripes.

8 Join both long open edges with running stitch, see Techniques page 178, and pull the thread to gather the strip so that it measures the perimeter of the bedspread.

9 Turn the bedspread right side up. Lay the gathered border along the top edge of the bedspread and machine stitch the two together, about ¼ in/0.75 cm inside the outer edge, as shown below right.

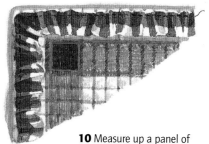

10 Measure up a panel of contrasting fabric for the backing. Join widths together if necessary. Add a ½ in/1.25 cm allowance all around. Cut out. Lay the front panel and interlining right side down. Lay the backing fabric right side up over it. Fold in the seam allowance all around the panel of backing fabric. Fold over the gathered border. Pin and baste. Hand sew around the perimeter of the backing panel, following the stitch line of the gathered border made on the top side of the bedspread, see detail above left.

6 Machine stitch along the lines of basting or tacking to join the two layers. Do not machine stitch around the perimeter, leave the basting stitches.

11 To make the eight bows, cut out 1 in/2.5cm wide strips of contrasting fabric on the bias. Fold each strip in half lengthways, right sides together and iron flat. Seam along the long edge. Turn right side out and iron flat. Arrange each strip in a bow and with a quilting needle hand stitch at the junction of each glasscloth or tea towel, piercing the interlining and the contrasting fabric to help secure the layers together.

7 To make the border, cut out enough strips of 2 in/5 cm wide contrasting fabric to measure twice the perimeter of the finished bedspread. Join the strips end to end. Fold the strips in half lengthways, right sides out and iron.

GLASSCLOTH OR TEA TOWEL BEDSPREAD

Materials

For a bed 5 ft/1.5 m wide
Basic sewing kit (see page 176)
15 standard-size glasscloths or tea towels
7 yd/6 m interlining fabric
8 yd/7 m contrasting fabric

①

③

④

⑤

① Children's bedrooms offer ample opportunity for soft furnishing treatments. In this room, very simple white-painted furniture is decorated with a gold star motif to echo the gray and white checkerboard floorcloth. The star theme is continued in a simple cotton squab cushion on the chair.

② In a loft or attic bedroom with a steeply sloping ceiling a simple pine bed constructed from timbers nailed to a head- and footboard is dressed with a Swedish-style canopy. Generous swathes of cotton *toile de Jouy* edged in red binding are draped from a central coronet that is fixed to the wall.

②

③ A brass bed fits snugly under the sloping ceiling of a top-floor guest bedroom decorated with a bold mix of black and white cotton *toile de Jouy* and plaids.

④ Smaller items of furniture such as footstools can be tight-covered with the help of a staple gun and the edges then neatened with braid or trim. Here, cotton *toile de Jouy* print edged in cotton rope picks up the main theme in a bedroom.

⑤ A baby's crib is beautifully loose-covered in a blue and white cotton stripe with a plain white border that matches the drapes. The panels that frame the crib are tied together at all four corners with little bows.

⑥ A collection of pressed, printed baby linens and a lambswool blanket edged in cotton are draped over the side of a crib, ready for use in a nursery room.

⑦ A detail of the pillowcase shown in picture 11; large- and small-scale checks mix happily with a lace trim.

⑧ Contrasting strongly with bold floral wallpaper, a single bed is given a stylish treatment. The quilt cover on the bed matches the draped overhead canopy of linen check edged in white cotton lace. The short end panel of the canopy, above the foot of the bed, is embellished with a piece of antique beadwork that comes from Eastern Europe.

9 10 A metal-framed bed is smartened up with antique linen slip-on covers. Panels of fabric were cut out according to the shape of the head- and footboards; after hemming, strips of linen were sewn at regular intervals around the edge of the panels and tied into bows. The slip-on cover at the head of the bed is personalized with an embroidered initial.

11 In a cozy cottage bedroom an old-fashioned iron bed with loose-covered ends looks completely at home. The heavy, checked quilt was discovered in a market. The dust ruffle or valance is made from a woven cotton sewn into neat kick pleats and the bedside tablecloth is fashioned from linen glasscloths or tea towels and topped with a piece of homespun linen.

8

9

10

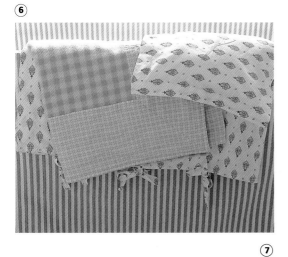

6

7

11

A simple wood frame covered in a cheerful, hard-wearing fabric provides storage space for toys and clothes in a child's bedroom.

2 Machine stitch the three panels together. For seaming, see Techniques page 179.

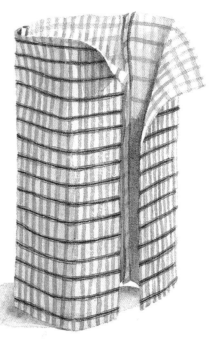

FABRIC-COVERED WARDROBE

Materials

Basic sewing kit (see page 176)
Wood frame
About 9 yd/8 m fabric
About 9 yd/8 m trimming tape
Template for scallops such as a plate or a cup
Marker pen

1 Measure the height (A) and width (B) of the back of the wood frame and add a ¾ in/2 cm seam allowance all around. Cut out a panel of fabric to this size. Measure up two more panels of fabric to cover the sides and half the front of the frame (C). The length of each panel will equal the height of the frame and the width will measure the depth of the frame plus half the width of the front, with an additional ¾ in/2 cm seam allowance all around. In this case the panel width was 37 in/94 cm.

3 For the front opening, make a ½ in/1.25 cm fold down either side, turn outward and iron down. Sew trimming tape over this to hide the raw edge. Sew trimming tape all around the bottom edge.

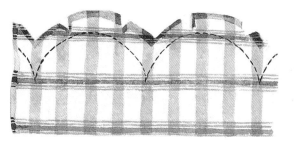

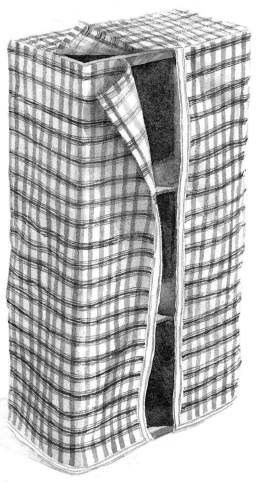

4 Measure the top of the frame and add a ¾ in/2 cm seam allowance all around. Cut out a panel of main fabric. Fold the seam allowance under on all four sides. With right sides together, pin and baste the roof panel to the top of the back and side panels and two halves of the front panel along the seam allowance fold. Hand sew together. Place the whole over the frame to check the fit.

5 To make the scalloped hood: cut out a piece of fabric 3 yd/2.75 m long and 18 in/45.5 cm wide. Fold in half lengthways, right sides together. Keeping the fabric square, use a template such as a plate or a cup and trace scallops about 9 in/23 cm wide and 8 in/20 cm deep with a marker pen.

6 Machine stitch along the line of scallops. Cut out ¼ in/ 0.75 cm outside the stitch line and turn right side out.

7 Iron flat and hand sew to the edge of the roof panel, making sure that the scallops are centered.

8 To make the ties: cut out four strips of fabric 20 in/ 50 cm long and 4 in/10cm wide. Fold each strip in half lengthways, right sides together. Machine stitch the long open edges together. Stitch at an angle on one end and trim off the excess fabric. Turn right side out and press.

Tuck in the ¼ in/0.75 cm raw edge at the open end of the tie and hand sew in pairs at regular intervals to either side of the front opening. Repeat for the remaining ties.

THE BATHROOM is often one of the most neglected areas in the home. All too often cold, clinical and often not designed at all, most bathrooms tend toward the functional. They are certainly rooms which are not softly furnished in the same way as other parts of the house. Window treatments are usually the main fabric consideration and as bathroom windows are frequently small and glazed with obscured glass, basic shades or blinds or simple short drapes or curtains are common.

However, as plumbing improves and bathtubs and showers become more sophisticated the bathroom is increasingly seen as a place to indulge oneself. Because the bathroom still tends to be one of the smallest rooms in the house it has to be planned to work ergonomically and practically. And even if it is not possible to rearrange the layout because of restrictions on plumbing, it is possible to make improvements in terms of the visual impact and overall comfort of the room by adding color, pattern interest and soft touches. In addition to soft furnishings there are all sorts of other items you might find in a bathroom, such as tissue holders, fabric-lined baskets or attractive containers for cosmetics. For more suggestions for accessorizing the bathroom see the chapter on Accessories, pages 148-73.

Bathrooms have a surplus of cold, shiny surfaces such as glossy tiles and gleaming chrome faucets or taps and shower heads and the lines of the bathtub, sink or basin are rather unyielding. Therefore this is an ideal place to use welcoming textures. Tones can be strong and patterns quite bold to create intimacy.

If you wish to enlarge your bathroom you should give careful consideration to planning, refurbishing and plumbing in order to maximize the available space. Work out a new arrangement as accurately as possible using a scaled floor plan and templates of existing and any possible new equipment. There are various clever ways of creating an illusion of greater space. You can use pale colors and light-reflecting textures such as mirrors either in the form of a whole wall of mirror panelling or with more modest mirror tiles. You should make sure that these are hung on a perfectly flat surface or else you will get a distorted reflection. If you use the same color on the floor, walls and bathtub panel then the effect will be to magnify the space. Any decorative scheme works around a predominant or main color.

Bathrooms

Opposite An old-fashioned bathtub is given a lavish treatment with a canopy of checked linen lined with white cotton. The long, narrow panel of fabric is suspended high up on the wall and drapes elegantly over a pair of large wooden bosses in a triangular configuration.

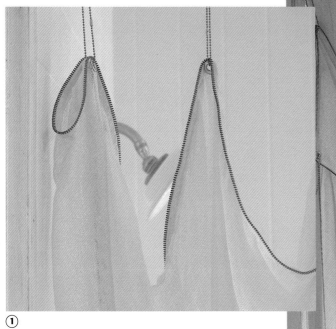

①

②

③

④

① Lengths of zippering edge a silk-textured shower drape fixed to the ceiling with chrome-beaded chains.

② A zipper-edged shower drape brings a modern touch to a traditional bathroom (detail shown in picture 1).

③ By means of special touch-and-close or Velcro tape which adheres to shiny surfaces such as porcelain, a wall-hung sink or basin in a bathroom is transformed with a gathered printed cotton skirt. This decorative treatment also provides useful hidden storage space.

④ White cotton terrycloth hangs from the ceiling to enclose a bathtub. It is lined with a layer of clear plastic to protect it from steam and splashes.

⑤

⑤ An elegant bathroom with a marble bathtub and a wall-mounted double sink or basin. The unyielding surfaces and terra-cotta floor tiles are softened by floor-to-ceiling drapes lined in *toile de Jouy* which hang from a wooden pole and bunch on the floor.

⑥ Stools and ottomans are useful items of furniture in the bathroom. Here a low stool is loose-covered with a panel of heavily embroidered antique peasant linen.

⑦ In an unadorned farmhouse bathroom the wooden window frame is painted to give it prominence. A practical Roman shade or blind made from homespun cotton is inset into the frame.

⑥

In the bathroom your choice of decoration may depend on the color of the bathtub, sink or basin, toilet and perhaps a bidet. The bathroom equipment may be a cold color such as a green or a blue, or possibly a strong, dark color such as burgundy or even black. Such dark colors are not an ideal choice for bathroom sanitaryware as they show up dirt. So if you are starting a bathroom from scratch select a more practical color. White is the classic choice, but there are also some ivory tones or "whisper" shades which have just a faint blush of color to create a less clinical feel. Or you may prefer some of the pastels now available. Whatever the color of the bathroom equipment, the decorative scheme should be worked around it and you may wish to co-ordinate, emphasize or overpower the main color by using deeper or lighter tones on other surfaces in the room.

You can follow the basic principles for color scheming just as well in the bathroom as for all the other rooms in the home, but you may need to link the scheme with another area, for example, if the bedroom and bathroom adjoin or if you want to have a bathroom or shower room to be all-of-a-piece with the hallway or landing from which it leads. This does not mean that the colors and materials you use have to be identical, although it helps to lay the same floor covering throughout. It is advisable to decide on the hard textures in the bathroom before you begin to add soft furnishings. Although tiled or part-tiled walls and floors are commonly found in the bathroom these harsh, cold textures are really only essential as a splash-back behind the sink or basin and around the top of the bathtub and in a shower enclosure. There are plenty of other alternatives, from vinyl finishes to three-dimensional paint finishes, for decorating bathroom walls as a background for additional

⑦

fabric treatments – but whatever your choice the wallcovering should be water-and steamproof and washable. Add soft, textural contrast, in the form of luxurious deep-pile towels with fringed ends or pillows or cushions covered in towelling and contrast trim upholstery and drapes with a cotton fringe, frills or braid. Make sure that the trim is of a similar fiber and weight as the main towelling or fabric; it must also be color-fast so that you don't have problems with puckering, shrinking or the color running during washing.

Fabrics in the bathroom should be damp-proof and mold-resistant, especially where shower drapes and window treatments over sinks or basins are concerned, as these are likely to get splashed frequently. Plastic is often used for shower drapes, but this has a rather rigid texture and does not hang well. You could be more imaginative and disguise a shower unit or enclose a bathtub with a fabric which co-ordinates or contrasts with the window treatment or the wallcovering, but you must choose a washable, shrink-proof, firmly-woven and smooth-textured cloth such as chintz, moiré, sateen, cotton, unbleached calico or linen.

(1)

(2)

(3)

(5)

(4)

(1) A plain cotton drape lined with clear plastic is fastened to a metal rail with ribbons.

(2) Panels of cream and gray linen cover a bathroom stool; the fabric is held in place with long ties.

(3) A wall-hung cabinet fronted with glazed doors is lined with miniature blue and white cotton gingham.

(4) Different checks blend happily together because they are linked by a blue and white color theme. The drapes are adapted from cotton sheets and topped by a simple gathered valance or pelmet.

(5) In a bathroom dominated by shiny textures the windows are given a minimal treatment and screened with a pair of simple roller shades or binds.

(6) A high folding screen is covered in cotton *toile de Jouy*. The patterned fabric complements the bold wallpaper and conceals a sink or basin.

(7) Delicate blue cross stitch decorates an antique lace-edged hand towel. You can give plain cotton towels a personal touch with a variety of embroidery stitches.

(8) Panels of gathered cotton voile are stretched inside the frame of a folding screen. The lightweight voile filters light and provides privacy in a bathroom. You can cover a screen frame with all kinds of fabrics.

Make a separate transparent layer of plastic lining and attach this at the top of the hanging with lining tape. The waterproof plastic lining and the outer layer of fabric can then be easily separated for cleaning and drying.

If your bathroom contains a dressing table or an old-fashioned sink or basin with rather unsightly plumbing on view then an all-concealing "skirt" in crisply pleated or softly draped fabric will disguise the underneath and simultaneously provide some useful storage space. The fabric skirt may be shirred onto wire and fixed to a frame or to the wall behind with hooks and eyes. Also, fabric-covered screens are appropriate in the bathroom – position them to conceal a toilet or bidet from the rest of the room or for temporarily draping clothes or towels over. For instance, cover the screen with light-diffusing fabric or make it reversible, using contrasting fabrics on each side.

For some, the idea of bathroom upholstery may seem far-fetched, but if you have the space then this will transform the setting into a comfortable interior and a place for relaxation. If space allows you might upholster a stripped pine, painted wood or metal *chaise longue* in

(6)

towelling or another soft, absorbent fabric such as a seersucker, or a brocaded cotton twill. Use a similar fabric to cover a large pillow or cushion placed perhaps on top of a linen box or pile loose pillows onto a Lloyd loom, cane or metal garden chair. Canvas, duck, cotton drill and calico or muslin are more unyielding fabrics and water tends to shrug off them so these lend themselves to bathroom upholstery.

If the bathroom has a recessed window then it may be possible to build a window seat. This might have a lift-up, padded top and provide an ideal place to store bath towels and other accoutrements. Upholster the padded top or the seat of a chair, stool or ottoman with matching or contrasting fabric; this should be treated for wet-resistance because it is likely to come into contact with water at some stage. The window seat can be softened with shaped and textured pillows for added luxury. If there is a radiator under the window you can cover it with a frame and form a window seat above, leaving a grille in the front to allow the hot air to circulate. This treatment would mean that the radiator could not be used for drying towels so you could install a ladder-type radiator against a wall.

⑦

⑧

BATHROOM STOOL

Materials

Basic sewing kit (see page 176)
Padded round stool
Main fabric
Staple gun
Contrasting fabric for corded piping

Bold brown and white striped cotton with a full gathered skirt smartens up an ordinary bathroom stool.

1 For the stool top: measure the circumference of the stool seat and cut out a circle of main fabric with an all-around 2 in/5cm allowance in order to attach the skirt. Position the circle of fabric right side up over the seat, keeping the pattern square. Staple tightly just below the rim of the seat. If you do not have a stool with a padded top, glue a circle of padding to fit the diameter of the top to soften the seat.

2 For the gathered skirt: measure the height of the stool from the floor to the seat and add an extra 1 in/2.5cm for a seam allowance at the top and turning under at the bottom. For the width, double the circumference of the seat to allow for gathering. Cut out a piece of main fabric to these measurements.

3 With the fabric right sides together, seam the two short sides together. Press. Baste two close rows of running stitch for gathering, see Techniques page 178, ½ in/1.25 cm from the top edge of the skirt panel; leave long thread ends.

4 Make up two lengths of corded piping in the contrasting fabric to go around the circumference of the stool seat and the hem of the skirt, see Techniques page 181.

5 Pin, baste and machine stitch the longer length of corded piping to the right side of the bottom of the skirt panel, ½ in/1.25 cm above the raw edge. Make sure that the two open edges of the piping are pointing toward the raw edge.

6 Turn the skirt wrong side out and press the ½ in/1.25 cm hem allowance along the bottom and the two layers of open piping edges inward. To neaten the bottom edge: overlock the three layers together and press again so that they lie pointing upward. (See Techniques page 180.) Pull the two long threads to gather the top of the skirt to the exact circumference of the stool seat.

7 Pin, baste and machine the piping to the right side of the gathered top of the skirt, ½ in/1.25 cm down from the raw edge. Make sure that the raw edges of the piping are pointing toward the raw edge of the gathered fabric. Join the ends of the piping neatly by hand.

8 Pin the gathered skirt to the seam allowance all around the seat of the stool, just above the staples. Lift the skirt up and flop it over the stool top in order to join the skirt evenly all around the seat. Work your way around the stool and adjust so that the skirt is attached evenly.

9 Continue to work on the stool with the skirt flopped over the seat so that the underside is visible. Make sure that all the raw edges, including the open edges of the piping are pointing in the same direction. Hand sew the gathered skirt to the seam allowance on the stool seat just below the cord, so that the piping sits neatly in between the rim of the seat and the top of the skirt.

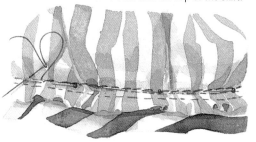

10 This striped skirt is simple to make and will add an elegant touch to a bathroom. The only complicated part is inserting the piping around the top of the skirt. For more information on how to produce a neat finish with piping, see Techniques, page 181.

Outdo

ORS

FURNISHING THE OUTDOORS may seem to be a contradiction in terms, but with the advent of fashionable patio and pool-side living, renewed enthusiasm for *al fresco* dining and the revival of the elegant turn-of-the-century picnic, all such moveable feasts deserve a beautiful setting. As conservatories and sun rooms appear in increasing numbers, fabric and furnishing details for garden rooms and outdoor settings have become scene stealers and an integral part of comfortable living. Not only is the garden often furnished nowadays, it is also accessorized, just like rooms inside the home. Vivid splashes of color can be provided in pillows or cushions, sunshades, upholstery, screens, tablecloths and napkins, as well as china, glass, candle holders and lanterns. And if you have a gazebo, a summer house or any other garden building, then you can decorate this with as much care, flair and style as you would an indoor room.

(1)

Previous page

Left Checked cotton decks a pretty pool-side setting.

Right On a breezy porch outdoor twig furniture is softened with quantities of cotton pillows that are covered in antique ticking fabrics.

(1) A vinyl pillow for outdoor use is loose-covered with cotton duck and fastened with ties.

(2) Large, pillows scattered over a bent-willow bench. The loose covers in antique and new checked cotton and striped fabric are a fresh mix of geometric patterns.

(3) Square panels of linen adorn a weatherproof teak rocking chair; the fabric is attached to the frame of the chair with ties and the back panel is stencilled.

(2)

(3)

When you are choosing fabrics, patterns and colors for conservatory, porch, patio, terrace or verandah furnishings, try to create a visual link between the house and garden.

Strong, fade-proof fabric such as canvas, duck, ticking or twill can be used to make a drape to cover an exterior door and protect a south- or west-facing entrance from hot sun. This can be drawn across the opening when the door is left ajar on summer days and will let in cool breezes while keeping out the sun. Stout, awning-type textiles can be used to cover lounging mattresses, deck chairs, club and director's chairs for use outside and to make seat and back pillows for wood, metal or plastic dining chairs. Be bold – the colors you use outdoors can be much stronger and the patterns much larger than those on fabrics for indoor use. And they are easier to choose since they don't usually have to co-ordinate closely with the surroundings. The wood or metal of a frame, the green of the grass, the stone or brick of the patio or terrace flooring and the wood of decking provide a neutral background which most colors and patterns can be set against. Colors can be scintillating in strong sunlight,

⑤

and provide a warm, friendly glow to evening entertaining. Consider the "sunshine" yellows, acid tangerines, vibrant reds, brilliant blues and rich greens. A riot of color often works just as well on the patio and against the cool green of the lawn as the exotic mixture of colors found in nature, where nothing ever seems to clash; yet indoors such a mix would be considered unacceptable and too difficult to live with.

Naturals and neutrals as well as paler colors can also work well outside. For instance, the sun-bleached faded shades of pale pastels or the natural tones of burlap or hessian, hemp, canvas and calico or muslin will look attractive as pillows on oiled wooden seats and benches, or rustic-style garden furniture. As an alternative, combine natural materials such as cane, rattan and bamboo furniture and screens with rich Indian red or jade-green fabrics for maximum impact; or with neutral shades and natural textures for a more restrained effect.

Flowers and foliage, blooming and trailing all over fabric and used to cover seating, tables and sun screens on the patio, porch or in the conservatory can also provide a wonderful link

⑥

④

⑦

④ Transform an ordinary hammock into something more luxurious by means of a loose-cover made of fine handkerchief linen and a loosely pleated skirt, then add pillows or cushions.

⑤ Temporary furnishings in a garden under a large canvas sunshade include a woven vinyl rug on the grass and casual throws and pillows.

⑥ A doorway screened by a drape consisting of a fabric panel with eyelets punched along the top that hook over masonry nails in the Gothic stone arch. The drape is held open at one side by a simple tie.

⑦ Wicker furniture can be made much more comfortable with a fabric treatment. In this case, wide-striped cotton upholstery softens the chair.

can bring an impression of continuous blooms into a small, over-shadowed town garden. A matching flowered sunshade, or garden parasol lined with sky-blue fabric will provide a patch of cool shade and, conversely, if lined with a sunshine yellow it will reflect heat and lend a feeling of warmth.

Ethnic patterns in earthy colors such as ochre, terra-cotta, gamboge and burnt umber will enhance streamlined wooden "steamer-style" furniture that is stained to match or contrast with the upholstery, though they can also be a perfect foil for white-enamelled cast-iron or aluminum pieces. Rich, deep plains, trimmed with a contrasting-colored fringe or striped piping will look sophisticated beside a pool or on a sundeck or to take to the beach on practical portable pieces.

Checks and stripes are attractive on all types of garden furniture. You can use them to loose-cover dining chairs to co-ordinate with a tablecloth and napkins, or adapt them to sunshades or to include in a picnic basket. The only real disadvantage of checks, tartans and stripes is that they can quarrel with the flowers and foliage in a richly planted area.

with the garden, especially if they echo a special planting scheme beyond, so helping to create an impression of a continuous vista. Paler, subtle full-blown florals will create an atmosphere of old-world charm on cane or rattan furniture and may be used to upholster a rocking chair on a verandah or a sunny porch; these look particularly appropriate in a cottage garden. Florals also look particularly good against lush greenery and on neatly manicured lawns, or to dress a pretty *al fresco* dining table. And they

(1) Beside an outdoor swimming pool a pair of metal *chaises* are made comfortable with padded covers in bright striped awning fabric. The tough fabric is rot-proof, which is important in a humid climate.

(2) The padded *chaise* covers are decorated with thin knotted ties which resemble buttoning. The ties are made with matching striped fabric cut on the cross.

(3) An inviting pool-side setting. The garden furniture is decked out in a summery display of crisp white and cheerful red cotton country checks and stripes.

(4) Table napkins converted into tie-on covers for a metal chair. Simple to make (see pages 144-5) and easy to wash, this is a novel idea for an open-air party.

(5)

(6)

(7)

(8)

(5) For a pool-side buffet an ordinary table is given a smart, instant treatment and covered with a floor-length cloth made of alternate strips of coral and white cotton that have been pieced together.

(6) Matching panels of hemmed red and white striped cotton piqué are fastened around a large rectangular squab on a reproduction classical garden bench.

(7) A detail of the seat squab on the same bench shows how two panels of striped fabric encase an inner covering of plain red and are fastened with ties.

(8) At either end of the seat is a back pillow or cushion in co-ordinating fabric with a striped border that has been neatly mitered at the corners.

1 To make the chair back use one napkin. Make two incisions in the top two corners of the napkin. The slits should be just longer than the size of the width of the cotton tape. With the napkin right side up finish the slits with buttonhole stitch, see Techniques page 179.

2 Take the same napkin; sew two lengths of tape, each 19½ inch/50 cm long in the two corners opposite the buttonholes. Sew two more lengths of tape on the reverse side of the napkin in the same two corners. To finish the ends of the tape make a double ¼ in / 0.75 cm fold. Press and hand sew.

3 Fold the napkin in half, right side out, over the top of the chair back.

4 Pull the cotton tape throught the buttonholes at the front and tie into a bow so that the napkin is secured to the chair back.

FOLDING CHAIR COVER
Materials

Basic sewing kit (see page 176)
Three napkins that are 2 in/5 cm larger than the seat of the chair and have finished edges
4½ yd / 4 m of 1 in/ 2.5 cm wide cotton tape
Thin foam pad, to fit the size of the chair seat

6 Position a thin foam pad over it. Pin and baste four more 19 in/50 cm strips of tape on both sides of the squab cushion where the back chair legs meet the seat.

7 Place another napkin right side up over the foam pad and machine stitch around all four sides, making sure that the cotton tape ties are secured inside the seam. Finish the ends of the ties as in step 2.

In an outdoor setting, a French sidewalk chair is given a fresh treatment – the seat and back covers are fashioned from ordinary table napkins.

5 To make the seat squab cushion, place one napkin wrong side up on a flat surface.

8 Place the squab or cushion on the seat and tie bows with the cotton tape to secure it to the chair back.

①

②

③

④

The guidelines on pattern size, shape and scale given for indoor treatments apply to the garden too. Bold designs look best on large items of furniture where the whole pattern repeat can be seen to advantage. Try them on garden *chaises*, for large loungers, for covering conservatory couches, on Hollywood-style swinging garden hammocks, to cushion big benches and for swathing large buffet tables.

Select fabrics for outdoor furnishings with care. Consider the type of use that they will receive. Make sure that fabrics covering pillows and upholstery are as hard-wearing, stain-resistant and snag-proof as those you would select for the living room. Accidents can happen outdoors too – consider flammability when choosing items to be sited near a barbecue, or if you propose to light the garden with candles and storm lanterns for evening entertaining.

Today there is a wide choice of suitable fabrics for outdoor use, including different weights of canvas (look for these in ships' chandlers), striped ticking and deck-chair canvas and awning fabrics – some have a plasticized finish. Many of these can be somewhat stiff and unyielding, and so are mostly suitable for items such as screens, windbreaks, hammocks and deck chairs. They are not pliable enough for fitted or loose covers nor drapeable enough for table furnishings. Traditional cottons, linens, linen unions, ribbed twill, some interestingly textured synthetics and even crisp chintz will drape well for cloths and tie-on loose covers, so long as they are of upholstery fabric weight.

If fabric is to remain outdoors overnight it needs to be damp-proof, and if it is to withstand strong sunlight it must be fade- and rot-proof. It makes sense to use loose or tie-on covers on garden chairs, sofas, benches and swings so that they can be removed for cleaning or drying in

⑤

case they have been inadvertently left out in a rain shower – and this means that they should be shrink-proof as well. Fabrics used for tablecloths, napkins, picnic sets and basket linings are more practical if they are washable and need little, if any, ironing. Some easy-wipe plasticized finishes may be more practical for items which are taken to the beach, lakeside or swimming pool, where sun oil, sand and grease are likely to take their toll.

⑦

⑥

① Cotton twill covers an outdoor table and chairs, providing a pristine setting for terra-cotta pots planted with miniature roses and antique china.

② A stone table covered with a fitted gathered cloth of cotton twill; the folding garden chairs are given a formal treatment with floor-length loose covers.

③ Buttoning is an easy way to add character to a pillow or cushion or a loose cover. Here, a cream cotton tufted button livens up a plain red pillow.

④ Assorted antique linen table napkins are simple to make and add a finishing flourish to a table setting. Use remnants of washable cotton and simply pull the fibers along the sides to make a fringed edge.

⑤ Laid out on a traditional American cotton tablecloth a spongeware jug and a bandana-type napkin create a pretty grouping on a duo-tone color theme.

⑥ An old-fashioned wooden knife box filled with cutlery and antique fringed napkins.

⑦ Homespun fringed napkins act as a nest for apples.

147

ACCENTS AND ACCESSORIES add finishing touches to a scheme and personality to a home. They can contribute to an interior in all sorts of ways – to soften a stark setting, add a sharp, colorful or shiny contrast to a dull background, enliven a bland setting, add warmth to a cold room or coolness to a hot one, pull a scheme together or help to set a specific theme.

But what exactly is an accessory? In terms of interior design it is an unusual item or a collection or group of carefully chosen possessions which are added to a room once decorating is complete – although a special accessory may also provide a trigger for a scheme or suggest an entire theme for a room. While pillows or cushions, bolsters, lamps and shades, towels, toiletries, picture frames and boxes are all separate items which can accessorize a room, fabric accessories also include the braids and trimmings on drapes or curtains, covers and upholstery, all of which add definition to a main item.

Acce

ssories

Soft accessories include most items that are made from textiles, from small personal items to grand table treatments, dressing-table and small side table covers. However, the color, choice of fabric and style of these more sizeable items should be integrated into the overall scheme and not added as an afterthought. For example, in the bedroom do not regard the bedding as an accessory – because the bed is an important part of the total room area the bedding is central rather than incidental to the overall theme. Likewise, in the dining room the table setting should relate to the rest of the scheme.

Some of the most popular and ubiquitous soft furnishing accessories are pillows and cushions which can be used in any room of the house. They can be tossed casually onto beds, couches or chairs or used as informal seat covers. Flat squabs will soften a hard wooden, cane or metal seat or in bolster form you can create comfortable arms and back for an unyielding seat. But they can also be more tailored and decorative and tied onto an upright chair with bows or tapes. Other applications include hanging squabs from a pole to form a back to a divan to convert it into a couch or to create a soft headboard. You can pile pillows or cushions on the floor to provide supplementary seating or quilt them into a box-shaped squab to sit snugly inside a wickerwork chair.

Previous page

Left Ornate glass-column lamps with formal pleated and frilled shades made of silk taffeta.

Right A generous scattering of pillows on a deep sofa that is tight-covered in a woven cotton check.

(1) White cotton embellished with black wool appliqué.

(2) A silk pillow with appliqué birds sits on a *chaise longue* upholstered in vivid striped silk.

④

③ A small oblong silk pillow on a French couch.

④ Plain wool intricately decorated with black braiding.

⑤⑥ Fabric remnants and plenty of gold braid are hand-sewn onto pillows to represent regal coats of arms.

⑦ Pillows made of heavy cotton ottoman cloth bordered in pale gray ultrasuede to complement a bedspread.

⑥

1 Cut out a 19 in/48 cm square piece of main fabric for the back, this is panel A. Cut out two 10 in/25.5 cm square pieces of main fabric for two front panels, these are panels B and E. Cut out two 10 in/25.5 cm square pieces of contrasting fabric for two more front panels, these are panels C and D. Iron a ½ in/1.25 cm seam allowance around all four sides of each front panel. Open out the folds.

3 Pin and baste an appliqué motif onto the right side of each of the two contrasting fabric front panels, C and D. Overlock by machine, see Techniques page 180.

4 Lay the front panels B and C, right sides together, and machine down the ironed fold. Repeat with panels D and E.

Remnants of all types of fabric can be used to make original pillows or cushions.

2 Press two scraps of fabric onto adhesive webbing or fabric stiffener. Draw on appliqué motifs and cut out.

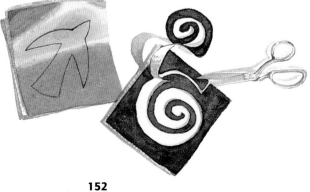

5 Open out the front panel B, C. Place right side down and pin and baste the seam to the left.

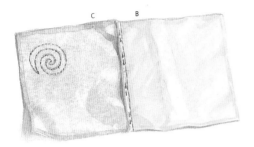

6 Open out the front panel D, E. Place right side down and pin and baste the seam to the right.

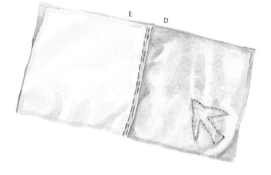

7 Place the front panels B, C and D, E right sides together and machine stitch, with the seam lying upward. Press the front panel.

8 Place the front panel (B, C, D, E) and the back panel A right sides together. Machine stitch along the pressed fold lines on all four sides, leaving an opening in the middle of the fourth side.

9 Turn right side out and press. Insert the square cushion or pillow pad and hand sew to close the opening, see Techniques page 178.

APPLIQUE PILLOW OR CUSHION

Materials

Basic sewing kit (see page 176)
18 in/45.5 cm square pad
Main fabric for back and two front panels
Contrasting fabric for two front panels
Scraps of fabric for appliqué
Adhesive webbing or iron-on fabric stiffener

(1)

(3)

1. Use trimmings and braids to embellish pillows or cushions. Old-fashioned wooden toggles edge a woven chenille pillow; underneath, a patterned linen cushion is trimmed with a thick cotton fringe.

2. A printed Fortuny fabric pillow double-edged in linen with a rope trim and a cotton bobble fringe.

3. Adorning a modern chair with an ash frame, a large cotton pillow is edged in a tasselled cotton fringe.

4. For an original edging, small holes were drilled into miniature sea shells which were then handsewn to border a linen pillow.

5. One of the advantages of pillows is that different shapes, sizes, colors and textures may be mixed together; this assortment includes a plain-edged bolster, cushions with piped edges and a pillow in the middle with a rich cotton tasselled fringe.

6. Luxurious green velvet is finished with a thick matching cotton fringe.

7. Using more than one trimming on a single pillow or cushion gives added textural interest. Here, a ruffle-edged silk pillow backed in a plaid silk taffeta has a double trim made of twisted rope.

8. A printed cotton damask pillow is attached to a stool by means of cotton rope ties with tasselled ends.

9. Antique textile panels that are bordered in linen and then edged in a chunky cotton fringe make beautifully textured pillows.

(2)

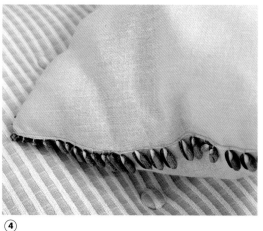

(4)

(5)

⑥

The shapes, sizes and designs are endless, from giant mattress-size cushions to tiny love pillows or herbal pillows stuffed with sweet-smelling lavender or *pot pourri*. Square, oblong, circular, conical, oval or cylindrical, the choice is enormous and you will achieve maximum impact by mixing shape, size, color, texture, pattern and plain effects in one group. For a neat, tailored look try a square shape covered in striped ticking with smart buttons. For something more traditional a square, circular or oblong shape covered in brocade with a corded or fringed trim is appropriate. Or try dressing up a pillow or cushion rather like a package by draping it with fabric and then tying it with cord, braid or other type of trimming. This treatment works particulary well with bolsters which you can wrap in a generous amount of fabric, leaving a surplus at each end to bunch up rather like a Christmas cracker.

The fabrics that you select for pillows or cushions can be as varied as you like, but you should avoid using very fragile textiles which might pull apart at the seams. If you wish to use a delicate covering such as lace or muslin or calico it will need to be backed with a stronger, fabric such as a close-weave cotton. Many different hand- or machine-stitching techniques can be used to enhance the main covering – embroidery, appliqué and quilting will all add an extra dimension. The edging can be equally varied, from cord-edged trim, simple single or more pronounced double piping, a basic flange or a scalloped edge, to any one of a number of braids, fringes, tassels and borders.

The actual filling of a pillow or cushion should be enclosed with an inner cover or casing made from lining fabric such as muslin or calico, ticking, cambric or down-proof fustian. This inner casing remains intact when the outer one is removed for cleaning and it also prevents the filling from escaping. The best fillings are pure down or down and feather mixes. These make soft, comfortable pillows or cushions which can be plumped up time and time again and do not lose their shape; they will also provide enough solidity for sitting on. Plastic or latex foam chips are less expensive and a sensible choice for pillows or cushions which will be used outside. However, they do become lumpy in time and also tend to disintegrate into crumbs. Firmer foam slabs or blocks can be used for unusually shaped or tailored cushions and cut down to the required size with a sharp craft knife.

⑦   ⑨

⑧

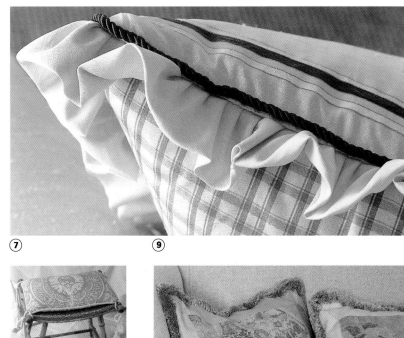

① Rattan is softened with cotton and lace pillows.

② Fine lace provides an appropriate edging for pristine white cotton pillows.

③ Two shades of cotton seamed together make a smart treatment for a dining chair. For the matching, frilled-edge pillow, the same colors are reversed.

④ A cotton ticking pillow with Turkish corners is banded with ticking cut on the cross and handsewn with a double row of stitching.

⑤ Cotton ticking upholstery on a rectangular footstool, with self-piping around the top and cotton braid edging around the bottom.

⑥ A buttoned, black horsehair squab cushion makes a wrought-iron stool more comfortable to sit on.

As well as applying fabric onto a backing you can decorate textiles for accessories with stencils. Stencilled patterns add character and interest to many items and can help to pull together a scheme by repeating a design motif on one surface which appears on another. You can buy pre-cut stencils or else cut your own with a stencil kit – you might like to try and echo a pattern from an existing wallcovering, ceramic tiling or a flooring across the bottom of a roller shade or blind. Or add a stencilled design to a bedcover or fabric-covered headboard to repeat a motif from the drape or curtain fabric, rug or carpet, or use stencils on pillows or cushions, screens or to decorate tablecloths and napkins. Use special fabric paints for stencilling on cloth, available from good art and craft shops.

The textile should have a fairly smooth or matte surface – calico or muslin, closely woven cotton or linen, canvas or curtain lining are suitable. Shiny surfaces such as glazed chintz, moiré, brocade and silk cannot be successfully stencilled. If in doubt, test the paint on a scrap of fabric before you start and whichever fabric you decide to use pre-wash it to remove any size and iron it so that you have a perfectly flat surface to work on. Follow the manufacturer's instructions in order to complete the stencil.

As with all fabrics in the home it is wise opt for color-fast and fade-proof fabrics, in particular where washing or cleaning will be required fairly regularly. The advantage of making your own accessories is that there is an almost infinite selection of textiles to choose from. For small items, fabrics do not need to be as strong as those used for larger-scale drapes and curtains, loose covers or upholstery, so you do not need to confine yourself to furnishing fabrics. Experiment with dressmaking fabrics as well as all sorts of dress trimmings such as ricrac braid, velvet and machine-embroidered ribbons. Save offcuts from dressmaking or hunt through remnant counters for material. You can also adapt silk and other types of scarves to make accessories – sew them together to make a tablecloth, a throw or an unusual bedcover. Or take glasscloths, tea towels or table napkins and join them together with bold blanket stitches to create a decorative cloth.

Trimmings, cords and fabric borders are accessories which can be used to add emphasis and style to drapes and curtains, shades or blinds, over-bed treatments, tablecloths, upholstery and loose covers or used to edge smaller items such as pillows or cushions and lampshades. The contrast between the main

④

⑤

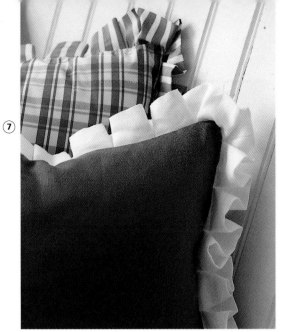

⑦

⑧

⑦ Contrast box-pleated edges lend a formal finish to a pair of pillows or cushions.

⑧ Quilted cotton *toile de Jouy* has been edged with a black cotton rope. A contrasting trim helps to define the outline of the main furnishing fabric.

⑨ On an antique corner chair a cotton buttoned squab cushion is outlined with narrow black rope.

⑩ White quilted matelasse cotton is beautifully edged using a wide ticking stripe which has been neatly mitered at the corners.

⑥

⑨

⑩

(1) A simply tailored pillow made from a striped linen is an ideal accessory for a modern setting.

(2) Woven raffia is edged with a natural linen flap to provide a beautifully textured pillow.

(3) Fall or autumn shades of natural wool make elegant pillows which have been self-piped.

(4) Antique tapestry makes for richly textured pillows; these are edged in a twisted cotton rope border.

(5) A subtle striped silk pillow contrasts happily with a contrasting plain raw silk.

(6) Chocolate-brown striped cotton is cut on the cross to give a decorative trim to a pillow.

(4)

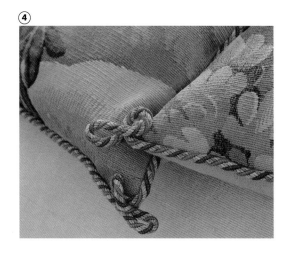

(5)

(2)

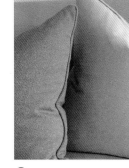

(3)

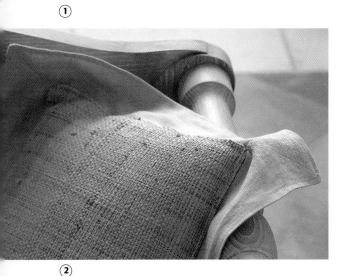

(1)

fabric and the trimming can be bold and dramatic – perhaps a striped border against a patterned fabric or vice versa, two different patterns used to accent each other or contrasting textures such as silk braid on muslin or calico. You may prefer an understated look so try a slightly deeper or paler value of color against an elegant faded fabric, a pastel trim on a subtle floral, a silk bullion fringe emphasizing the richness of velvet drapes or a simple stripe against a toning plain fabric. Many fabric manufacturers produce co-ordinating trimmings including fringes, tassels and braids in the same color palette as their textiles so you should have no difficulty in color-matching, although it is more fun to do something original and select an unusual trimming yourself. First decide just how eye-catching the border is to be – is it intended to be a simple edging and help to outline a basic shape or will it be a stronger statement? Whichever you choose, the border must appear to be an integral part of the finished look; like a frame it will enhance and define the item it surrounds and can help to improve proportions visually. Borders do not have to be made from flat fabric and may be raised and even wadded. You can roll stuffing into long sausage shapes

and wrap this in fabric for trimming bedspreads, heavy drapes and very bold table covers. These heavy borders add weight and help to improve the way that the fabric falls; on the practical side they block out drafts and are sometimes used on door drapes. You can make effective outlining treatments with piping, braids, cords, baubles and beads or make a simple border with special fabric paint and a stencil. Among the many trimmings available are choux rosettes, knife-pleated rosettes and ready-made frills and bows; these can contrast in color and texture with a main fabric or echo the overall effect.

(6)

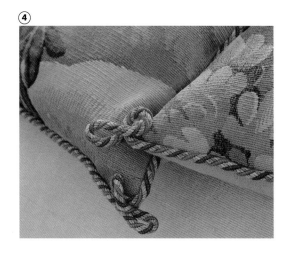

WOVEN PILLOW OR CUSHION

This pillow or cushion can be made from narrow strips of any kind of fabric, including ribbon and tape.

Materials

Narrow strips of fabric in two contrasting colors
Lining fabric
Backing fabric
Pillow or cushion pad

Decide on the size of pillow or cushion you require. Divide the width of the strips of fabric into the overall width of the pillow or cushion. To make a 15 in/37.5 cm square pillow you will need five strips of 3 in/7.5 cm fabric in each contrasting color.

1 Cut five strips of fabric in each contrasting color. Each finished strip should be 3 in/7.5 cm wide and 16 in/40 cm long. For this pillow or cushion hand-woven strips with finished edges

were used. If you use ordinary fabric strips with raw edges, cut out strips 4 in/10 cm wide. Place each strip wrong side up, make a double ¼ in/0.75 cm fold down each long edge and hand sew neatly.

2 Cut out the lining fabric to measure 16 in/40 cm square and lay flat.

3 Lay five strips of one color square over the lining.

4 Weave the strips of fabric in the contrasting color through the fabric strips positioned in the previous step so that they form a checkerboard pattern. Pin in place and baste around the perimeter.

5 Cut out the backing fabric to measure 16 in/40 cm square. Place the two squares right sides together and pin around all four sides. Machine stitch around the perimeter ½ in/1.5 cm in from the edge. Leave an opening on one side to turn right side out.

6 Turn right side out. Insert the pillow or cushion pad and close the opening with a neat hand stitch, see Techniques, page 178.

Checkerboard pillows or cushions made from interwoven strips of vegetable-dyed linen produced on a narrow loom.

ACCESSORIES

1. A pretty old button adorns a cotton country check.
2. Fine checked cotton lawn with self-buttoning covers a fitted pillow that sits snugly on a painted bench.
3. An assortment of different edgings: the striped cotton pillow at the top is trimmed with plain fabric; the middle pillow is piped and the lower cotton cushion is surrounded by a neatly mitered flap.
4. Large and small checks and antique *toile de Jouy* blend well together with a common color theme.
5. Strong red and white linen check provides a good foil for a collection of cotton *toile de Jouy* pillows or cushions in various shapes and sizes

(2)

(3)

(1)

6. A large, patriotic Stars-and-Stripes pillow on a corrugated cardboard armchair.
7. Woven cotton checks contrast in red and navy blue.
8. Antique cotton checks form a cheerful mix. Try to link pillows or cushions by color, pattern and texture to harmonize different fabrics.
9. Squab cushions are useful for softening hard seating. Here, woven cotton check is edged with antique cotton lace and attached to the legs of a painted Swedish chair with long ties.

(4)

You can also make trimmings easily at home from small scraps of fabric and give all sorts of large-scale soft furnishings unusual finishing touches. Buttons are other interesting extras and they can be covered in almost any type of fabric and then used to fasten upholstery, pillows or cushions. They also draw the eye to a particular area of a treatment, perhaps to emphasize the narrow point of a goblet heading or pinch-pleating on drapes or valances. This looks particularly effective if plain buttons are used against a patterned fabric and the same plain trim is used to outline the cornice or pelmet or valance edge and the tie-backs. On a practical note, borders and other trimmings are useful for lengthening drapes or covers which may have shrunk during cleaning or curtains that fall just short of the new windows after moving house. They can also add a new lease of life to tired soft furnishings or help to link them in with a new color scheme. Do not forget to test trimmings for color-fastness and make sure that they are shrink-proof as there is nothing more disappointing than a border that puckers up in the first trip to the cleaners or a fringe that droops.

Shelves used for storage do not have to be stark and utilitarian, in fact they offer potential for decorating and can become an integral part of the overall scheme of a room. The front edges of many shelves look grubby or uninteresting so you may wish to improve them. The treatment that you select will depend on the room and its styling. Try pinning a neatly frilled fabric valance to the edge of the shelf or slide a wire through a heading on the fabric and attach the wire to the edge of the shelf in several places – this looks crisp and fresh in a kitchen. You can also trim server or dresser shelves in the same way to give them a softer look, choose a fabric to echo the

⑧

⑤

⑥

⑦

⑨

colors and design of the china or pottery on display. If you wish to conceal items that are stored on shelves you can make miniature drapes to the desired depth and suspend them from a track fixed to the shelf edge.

For the bedroom something more elegant is called for so you could experiment with cotton pillow lace, narrow *broderie anglaise* edging, ricrac braid or simple swags of softly draped sheer fabric held in place with ribbon bows to hide the tacks or staples. The surface of the shelves can be given a soft touch with felt, green baize or almost any type of fabric; a plastic-coated or fully wipeable fabric makes sense for shelves which are subject to plenty of wear and tear. The fabric may be stuck or pinned on and the edge and finished with decorative brass-headed or other tacks. As an alternative, you can make a "sleeve" of fabric to enclose the shelf and then edge it with any of the trimmings suggested above. Use a fabric which is easy to clean and which will not shrink – glazed chintz oilcloth or firmly woven cotton is ideal – and avoid heavy or bumpy textures.

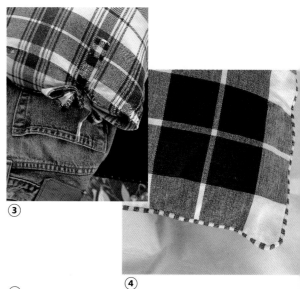

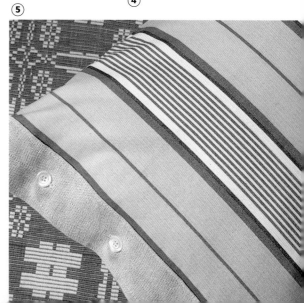

1. Create a casual look by fastening cotton pillow or cushion covers with simple ties.

2. Give a new look to cotton plaid pillows or cushions by cutting the fabric on the cross.

3. Ties for fastening loose covers can be made with either co-ordinating or contrasting fabric.

4. Striped piping complements a Madras cotton check pillow or cushion.

5. Different detailing – a neat buttoned edge in this case – on the same striped fabric used for the pillow shown in picture 1 gives a more formal look.

6. Red and white cotton mattress ticking has been used to make loose covers fastened with ties. These are a practical treatment for an outdoor setting as they can be slipped off easily for cleaning and winter storage.

7. A homespun blue and white squab with ruffled edges sits on a miniature child's chair with a rush seat.

8. A collection of pillows or cushions with buttoned closings and a gathered cotton ruffle serve to soften a stripped pine bench. If you use the same fabric texture – cotton in this case – you can mix patterns, geometrics and plains with ease.

9. Fresh red stripes are a good match for the wide, tailored flange of this cotton scatter pillow.

10. A cotton bedspread bought at an Egyptian market was turned into a summery pillow or cushion with an extra-wide gathered ruffle.

11. An antique kitchen waffle cotton glasscloth or tea towel with a woven edge makes a charming pillow cover which is finished with a fastening of old buttons. All pillows or cushions should have removable covers for laundering.

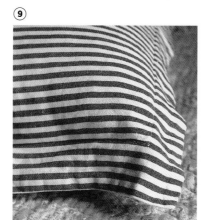

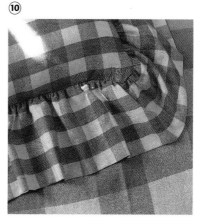

(4) Heavy burlap or hessian lends itself to box pleating. Ricrac edging outlines the lampshade top and bottom and the base is decorated with a fringe of miniature sea shells.

(5) A piece of antique linen sheeting becomes a tie-on cover to disguise an ordinary lampshade. It is finished with a cotton candystripe cut on the cross.

(6) In some cases you may wish to highlight the base of a lamp rather than the shade. To complement a patterned Chinese porcelain base a plain, tightly gathered silk shade is an appropriate choice.

(7)(8) In a contemporary-style loft or attic room modern and antique furniture co-exist comfortably. On the table, soft cream silk with a series of eyelets top and bottom is loosely gathered onto a metal frame to form a simple lampshade.

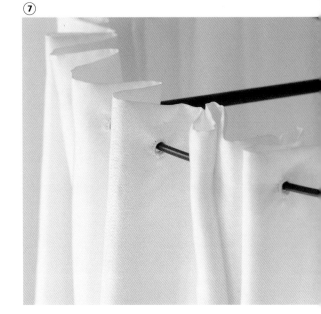

(1) Mauve chintz is tightly gathered and banded top and bottom to shade a wrought-iron lamp; the base is embellished with a matching frill.

(2) An antique tole tea caddy contrasts with a box-pleated cotton shade.

(3) Red cotton gingham gathered loosely and topped with a band of gimp makes a pretty, informal shade.

⑧

In any room of the house give careful thought to lighting and plan this at the outset – although the basic lighting fixtures and fittings should be an integral part of the initial scheme, lamps and their shades are classed as accessories and can be added once the room is complete, ideally to help enhance the overall style of the room. Note that fabric can often look quite different with light shining through it, rather than falling on it. When you are choosing or making your own fabric lampshades examine them both lit and unlit so that you can be sure they will work with your scheme during the daytime and at night.

Your choice and positioning of accessories is all-important. To give a room eye-catching finishing touches consider the basic principles of interior design and balance colors, contrast of texture and form and carefully combine patterned and plain surfaces. To add design interest to a room it is possible to use a group of plain accessories such as differently shaped and sized pillows or cushions piled on a couch, a chair or a bed. You can then group pictures or prints on a wall and link the frames in print-room style with garlands, ribbons or bows.

Although you will need to adopt different sewing techniques to create an array of accessories in the home, expensive equipment and sophisticated sewing machines are not mandatory because many items are quite simple to make and can be hand-sewn. If you are very inexperienced you can still make certain items such as wall hangings, screens and picture frames using non-fray fabrics which are simply stuck in place with a special fabric adhesive and require no stitching. Other projects require more specialist techniques, for example quilting to give extra bulk and warmth to a bedcover. Some accessories may call for decorative finishes such as piping, frills,

① A pair of ornate gilt wall sconces with pretty fine linen shades. The fabric is cut on the bias to create a skirted effect and the whole is fastened over an undershade with ties; the linen can be removed to shake off dust and for laundering.

② For a more formal lampshade the fabric can be tightly pleated. Here, a table lamp with a glass column base is shaded with crisp cotton pleats and given a finishing flourish with a silk ribbon tied into a bow.

③ On a writing table, a free-form metal base is topped with a simple shade covered in *toile de Jouy* which echoes the lining fabric of the drapes behind.

②

①

valances, cords, braids, scalloped edging or buttoning. Others may require embroidery skills, from simple drawn threadwork to tapestry, crewelwork and needlepoint. With some careful appliqué or stitching, you can revive an antique embroidery or other rich textile by attaching the old piece onto a new background fabric. Some traditional pieces of crewelwork, whitework, ethnic and even machine embroidery can be used in isolation or incorporated with a backing in this way. Beadwork is popular for covering stools and pillows or cushions, although it is also attractive suspended as cornices or pelmets and lambrequins as the weight of the beads helps the fabric to hang well. Berlin work – which was a forerunner of today's needlepoint kits – is often framed as a picture but it can also be used for covering the back or seat of a chair or to make an original footstool or hassock.

Patchwork is a popular sewing method and lends itself to all sorts of soft furnishings. Although it is most commonly associated with bedcovers and quilts, try making patchwork pillows or cushions, tablecloths and smaller items such as fabric bags for storing needlework equipment or use it to make a drawstring

patchwork bag lined with plastic for use in the bathroom. On the practical side, patchwork is an ideal way to use up small scraps of fabrics that may be left over from previous sewing projects.

Although screens were originally produced for practical purposes, to provide privacy and protect from drafts or strong sun, today they are often used as decorative accessories. The frame of a screen may be made of solid wood, open fretwork, cane, bamboo, wicker and even metal, but many types lend themselves to beautiful fabric treatments. A screen makes an excellent room divider: it may separate a dining room and living area; hide a washbasin or washstand or divide the dressing area from the sleeping area in a bedroom or seal off a cot or child's bed in a nursery. There are many ways of making screens, from restoring an old one to constructing a new one. Once the frame is complete the fabric may be shirred onto the top and bottom. Other types of screen have padding already mounted onto the frame which can then be covered with a fabric "sleeve" to completely envelop the frame. Or a textile can be fixed in place with decorative brass-headed upholstery tacks or ordinary tacks which can then be covered with gimp, ribbon or braid.

Table covers also offer scope for decorative trims. Any raised, flat surface, whether a rusting garden table, a well-worn trolley, an unsightly laminated table or a piece of rough chip- or particle-board of suitable height can be transformed into a table simply by covering it with attractive fabric. To make a simple cover take a pair of scissors and cut a circular, square, rectangular or oval piece of fabric. Then hem, fringe or trim the outer edge and simply throw it across the table to fall to the floor on all sides. Or you can create a layered look with a main cloth topped with one or more shorter overcloths.

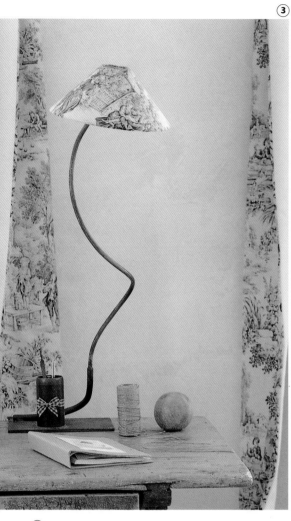

(4) A metal lamp base with a coolie shade is given a smart, cream silk trimming.

(5) Basic lampshades that consist of a simple cone shape are available in all sorts of sizes and thicknesses. Here, a thin card shade has been carefully covered with a piece of antique embroidered linen. When lit, the bulb inside diffuses soft light through the fabric to show up the delicate embroidery stitches on the fabric in an attractive silhouette.

(6) A plain fabric lampshade is given an original touch with a length of natural-fiber string that is coiled into loops and glued into place.

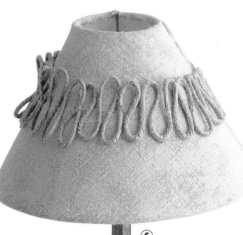

1 Cut out a length of main fabric 68½ in/174 cm long and 14 in/35.5 cm wide. Cut out a length of silk 68½ in/174 cm long and 9 in/23 cm wide.

2 Place the length of silk right side down and iron in a ¼ in/0.75 cm fold along the long edge.

3 Turn the silk over so that it is right side up. Place the folded edge over the bottom edge of the main fabric, which should be right side up. Overlap by ¼ in/0.75cm. Machine stitch together just inside the ironed fold. Press.

A box-pleated lampshade made in a saffron-yellow cotton adds a splash of color to a small table arrangement.

4 Fold and iron a ¼ in/0.75 cm seam allowance down each side of the joined strips

5 Fold back the silk lining all the way around the tube so that a ¾ in/2 cm strip of main fabric is visible above. The silk lining should stop 3¾ in/9.5 cm short of the top edge of the main fabric.

Fold the whole panel in half, right sides together and machine stitch along the ironed fold lines to produce a fabric tube with a diameter of 68 in/172.5 cm. Press.

PLEATED LAMPSHADE

Materials

Basic sewing kit (see page 176)
A lampshade frame with a 7 in/17.5 cm top diameter, a
14 in/8.75 cm base diameter and 9 in/23 cm height.
2 yd/1.75 m main fabric
2yd/1.75 m cream silk for lining
Fabric adhesive

6 Fold the top 2 in/5 cm of main fabric down to overlap the silk lining by ¼ in/0.75 cm and baste or tack the two layers together.

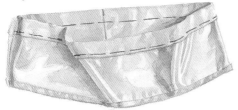

Turn right side out and press the top and bottom edges of the tube.

7 To make the pleats: fold a series of pleats along the top edge, so that each full pleat measures 1½ in/4 cm and each half pleat ¾ in/2 cm. Pin the pleats in place as you go until the circle is complete. Baste or tack the pleats 2 in/5 cm from the top to coincide with the join of the silk lining. Remove the pins.

8 Machine stitch along the line of basting or tacking. Place over the lampshade frame and glue from the inside to secure.

9 To make the bow: take a strip of main fabric 68 in/ 172.5 cm long and 2 in/5 cm wide. Right side down, make double ¼ in/0.75 cm folds along each long edge.

Fold both the short ends in the same way. Miter the corners, see Techniques page 180; press all the folds inward. Wrong side up, machine stitch around all four sides of the strip inside the ¼ in/0.75 folds.

10 Tie the strip around the top of the lampshade in a bow to conceal the line of machine stitching securing the pleats.

ACCESSORIES

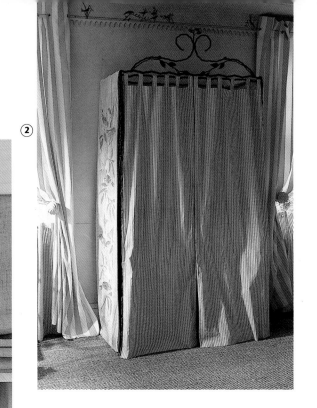

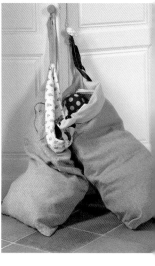

4. It is easy to transform accessories with fabric; this antique sewing box is covered in cotton *toile de Jouy*.

5. To hide the contents of a china cupboard, you can hang panels of fabric on tacks or a wire inside the doors. The doors are screened with cotton panels.

6. Hard-wearing stow-away bags for children's toys are useful items; burlap or hessian is an ideal fabric to choose and you can line the bags with a cotton print.

7. In a French winery, bottles of wine are encased in cotton-lined burlap or hessian sleeves, each with a specially designed opening to reveal the label.

8. Circles of cotton are secured to jar lids with raffia.

9. Cocktail coasters fashioned from printed cotton.

10. Antique linen bags hang on a traditional peg rail.

1. Raffia shades or blinds with cotton binding provide an attractive alternative to solid wardrobe doors.

2. You can use fabric hangings to disguise storage space or adorn a structure such as this wardrobe; hand-painted cotton panels hang at the sides and a drape with a looped heading is attached to the front.

3. In a loft or attic study a cupboard is given an original treatment; the doors are covered in printed cotton to match the walls and the interior is filled with neatly stacked boxes.

You can ornament tablecloths with embroidery, cutwork, appliqué, drawn threadwork or crewel. In a garden room, cloths do not need to be floor-length or finished with a fringe or a frill. For instance, a less formal, shorter circular cloth looks delightful with a stencilled floral border just above the hem. A printed cotton cloth with a tiny frill of lace peeping from underneath may be pretty in a bedroom, or try a cheerful checked gingham with a scalloped or castellated edge over a plain toning underskirt for a crisp treatment in the kitchen. You do not always need to trim a cloth, instead merely fold it to create various effects. For example, sew simple kick pleats at the corners of a short cloth to flatter the legs on a square table or box pleats around the edge of a piped circular tablecloth.

Small, left-over pieces of fabric can be used in all sorts of ways to create attractive finishing touches or hand-made gifts. The possibilities are endless – there are cosmetic bags, drawstring shoe bags, pomanders and herbal or lavender bags, while strips of padded fabric with inside pockets can be rolled up and neatly tied for storing jewelry. You can try covering a photograph or a mirror frame, a special photograph album, diary or book with fabric, or transform a plain noticeboard with cloth and overlay garden trellis or lattice ribbon or tape to hold the notes in place. For the table, use remnants to make napkins or napkin "rings" which can be simply tied or fastened with ordinary dressmaking buttons in interesting textures such as metal, glass or ceramic and perhaps make a matching fabric envelope to keep folded napkins in. Oven gloves, aprons for the kitchen or garden with generous pockets, tray cloths or simple runners to protect wooden surfaces and coffee, tea pot and egg cosies will provide inspiration. In the bedroom you can revive the idea of a nightdress or pyjama case and make a personalized gift for a child.

7

8

9

10

① A remnant of cotton *toile de Jouy* left over from a larger soft furnishing project is used to line a dog bed and given a ruffled edge.

② Rufus approves of his striped cotton-lined bed.

③④ Open shelves in a small bedroom concealed with a pair of cotton check drapes and topped with a narrow scalloped cornice or pelmet of woven check that has been painstakingly edged in antique white linen.

⑤ You can make all kinds of accessories with left-over pieces of fabric which you should not discard. A basket holds antique linen cocktail napkins embroidered with cross stitch.

Baskets, trugs and hampers of all shapes and sizes can be used for many purposes from storing logs, carrying food and utensils on a picnic to storing jewelry on the dressing table. Often they are improved with lining and you may select the fabric to co-ordinate with other items in the room or to link with the purpose of the basket, such as a floral or vegetable print fabric lining for a garden trug. The actual choice of fabric must also be practical. The inside of a log basket will be subject to rough treatment so a waterproof, heavy-duty canvas or plasticized fabric is appropriate. Any lining should be washable and cut to generous proportions so that it fits quite loosely. Fix the fabric by means of large, long basting or tacking stitches or with decorative ties, ribbon or tape.

Boxes, trunks and drawers can also be lined with cloth and you can add a herb sachet in matching fabric for freshness and fragrance. It is impractical to have loose linings in these situations as they may ruck up and catch when the box or drawer is opened and closed. You can simply stick a fabric lining in place and if it becomes stained you can rip it out and replace it with a new one. Plasticized fabrics and oilcloths offer practical, wipeable linings.

6 Very small-scale navy cotton gingham gives a pretty edge to a white cotton piqué placemat.

7 Hand towels of linen and waffle cotton are embroidered with red cross-stitch hearts.

8 Checked cotton sponge bags with draw-string ties are useful accessories in the bathroom, or for travelling.

9 As part of an attractive tablescape various objects, including a diary, a vase and some matchboxes, are covered in blue and white gingham.

10 Pin cushions made of antique woven cloth beside quilted lavender bags.

11 Transform an ordinary box by covering it with fabric.

Techn

iques

Most of the projects featured

in this book look smart and sophisticated, but in the main they are not difficult to make and they involve quite basic sewing skills which are explained fully in this chapter. Before you embark on any home sewing project you will need adequate and well-lit space in which to work. It is essential to have a large, flat surface on which to cut out fabric. A large dining or kitchen table can be pressed into service; protect the surface with layers of newspaper or a cloth to avoid damage. As an alternative, use a large piece of chipboard or laminate to cover an existing table. Avoid cutting out and pinning on the floor, particularly if it is carpeted.

If you are a beginner, avoid the temptation to start with more advanced sewing projects such as drapes or curtains with opulent headings, shades or blinds, or loose covers. Instead begin with a simple project and graduate to something more complicated once you have gained experience and confidence.

Basic Sewing Kit

As with any kind of home hobby it pays to buy the best tools and equipment that you can afford. Good sewing scissors are essential. Work with a sharp pair of proper cutting-out shears which have slightly curved handles, a medium-sized pair of dressmakers' scissors and a small pair of embroidery scissors. Pinking shears are useful tools for neatening raw edges. All sewing scissors require occasional sharpening and it is advisable to have them professionally ground.

Measuring and marking tools are equally important. For measuring up, a wooden yard or a metre stick is invaluable when working with large amounts of fabric for drapes or loose covers. A metal or wooden school ruler is useful for smaller work. A good tape measure is crucial and should have a stiffened end. A retractable 5- or 7-yard or extendable metre rule is helpful if you need to measure up very large windows. You may need several kinds of paper for measuring up larger items. Graph paper is useful for plotting designs or scaling patterns up and down. Use special pattern paper for cutting out or making templates. For marking up, tailor's chalk is ideal for making easy-to-remove marks on fabric; different colors are available. Marker pens are useful but the marks may be difficult to remove unless they are water-soluble.

Always use good-quality steel dressmaking pins as they won't mark the fabric. Glass-headed pins in several colors are useful when working on dark or heavily patterned fabrics; they are very sharp so take extra care. Never leave pins in work for an indefinite time or they will leaves holes in the fabric. Pins stored in a tin or box provided for the purpose will become blunt less quickly than those kept in a pin cushion. Keep a comprehensive selection of needles which includes bodkins for

threading, large darning needles and assorted sizes for general work. There are also special curved needles for upholstery and others for buttoning. Replenish needles and pins regularly as blunt or rusty ones will mark your fabric and bent needles are impossible to work with. Keep a thimble for hand sewing, particularly for heavy or coarse fabrics. Test the thimble for size and choose a metal one to protect your middle finger. For machine sewing, keep a stock of needles of assorted types and sizes (these change according to the type of fabric you are sewing or the foot that you are using). The needles must fit your particular machine, so refer to the manufacturer's instructions.

In order to join fabric together or hold it in place you will need to use sewing threads, adhesives or other forms of fixing. It is essential to use the correct thread for the job. Use basting cotton for basting. When sewing synthetic fabrics use a synthetic thread; do not use such threads on natural fibers such as cotton, silk or linen as they are strong and will damage the cloth. Use cotton thread on cotton and linen thread on linen. Do not use cotton threads on synthetic fabrics as they may shrink and can cause the work to pucker. If you are working with silk try to use a silk thread or a natural fiber thread. Always check the weight of the thread. For general use and for medium-weight fabrics choose a medium-weight thread. For voiles, sheers, nets, muslins and other fine fabrics use a lighter gauge thread. Choose strong threads for heavy-weight fabric. Try to color-match threads and fabric. For a patterned cloth match the thread to the most dominant color and choose a tone darker than the fabric as it will appear lighter when stitched. When machine stitching always wind the same color thread onto the bobbin and select the appropriate tension on the machine. Test several lines of stitching on a spare piece of fabric before you begin sewing.

In some cases fabric can be glued together with an adhesive, for instance to stick trimming in place on a hard cornice or pelmet, to trim a shade or blind or attach braid, ribbon or gimp in position to hide a join on a fabric-covered wall or to embellish a lampshade. Special fabric adhesives are sold under various brand names. These may mark or discolor the cloth so joins should be disguised with suitable trimming.

A staple gun can be an extremely useful tool for fixing or gathering fabric, either permanently or temporarily. A heavy-duty model will staple and pleat thick fabrics and take several thicknesses of cloth. Left-handed models are also available.

Various fastening devices are available for closing seamed openings. Zippers should be of the correct weight and size according to the fabric used. Do not mix fibers – use a natural-fiber zipper with natural-fiber cloth and a synthetic zipper with synthetic cloth. Match the colors and select the correct weight and shade of thread.

Hooks and eyes and old-fashioned poppers or snap fasteners are suitable for closing loose covers and pillows or cushions. These are often sold in strips mounted onto fray-free binding which can be sewn into an opening so that the fasteners automatically align correctly.

Touch-and-close or Velcro tape is a another means of fastening; two strips of nylon tape with miniature hooks key together. It is available in different widths and can be stitched into place on fabric or stuck to a hard surface such as a wall, a piece of furniture, a cornice or pelmet board so that fabric will adhere and may be easily removed for laundering. Try to match the tape closely in tone to the main fabric. Other methods of closure include buttons which can be secured with buttonholes (see page 179) or rouleau fastenings or frog fastenings. Simple fabric ties, braid and ribbon are further attractive ways to hold fabric in place.

Other useful items to keep in a basic sewing kit include a seam ripper which is a small tool used for unpicking seams and stitches quickly. For those who are short-sighted, an embroiderer's magnifying glass can be very helpful for examining detailed work. And a weight is practical for preventing heavy or slippery fabric from sliding off the cutting table. You can buy this or make your own easily by wrapping a brick or any other small, heavy object in a piece of blanket, batting or wadding and then covering the whole with fabric; attach a fabric handle for easy manoeuvring.

Although some of the simpler, small-scale projects in this book can be hand sewn, a basic sewing machine is required for most items. For making sizeable soft furnishings such as drapes or loose covers a machine is an essential aid. If you are buying a new machine an electrically operated one is ideal as it leaves both hands free to control the work. Make sure that you fully understand how it operates. Practice using different attachments and learn how to thread up and change needles and feet to suit the thread and fabrics you plan to use before you tackle a project using substantial amounts of costly fabric. Look after your machine well; store it in a warm, dry place. Always remove the cable when not in use or the motor could burn out. Clean and oil regularly and have it professionally serviced from time to time.

Fabric should always be well pressed as this facilitates sewing enormously. Press each stage carefully as you work; this is particularly important with seams and hems. It is also essential to iron out any creases or folds in the fabric before you start working on it. Always check the fiber content of the fabric before pressing and make sure that the iron is on the correct setting. Some fabrics should not be pressed with a steam iron or they will shrink or flatten, others respond well to pressing through a damp cloth. If in doubt, experiment on a small spare piece of fabric first.

Fabric Facts

All fabrics used for the projects featured in this book should be pre-shrunk and fade-resistant. Flame-retardant fabrics and upholstery fillings have legislation governing their use in many countries; obtain advice from a retailer.

Check that any printed pattern is aligned correctly on the weft grain otherwise it will not hang straight when made up into drapes and ensure that the pattern is in register and not smudged where one color overlaps another.

All drapes are improved with a fixed or detachable lining. (Only sheers should not be lined.) Lining helps the drape to hang better, it blocks out unwanted light and protects the main fabric from sun and fading, condensation and dirt. Cotton sateen is the most common lining fabric. Its closely woven, slightly shiny surface shrugs off dirt and dust. It is available in varying widths and colors. Choose a tone as close to the background of the main fabric as possible. Insulated linings are also available; there is a thermal variety which is a mix of cotton and acrylic or a more expensive aluminum-coated lining which reflects heat in summer and keeps heat in during the winter. So-called "black-out" or 'dim-out' lining is available in neutral shades; it has thermal qualities and totally excludes light. For a detachable lining you will need a special drape lining tape as well as the heading tape. Fixed linings are sewn into the drapes and do not require a separate heading tape.

Interlinings have a non-woven construction and so cannot be washed; always dry clean. They give more bulk and thermal qualities to drapes, quilts and bedcovers, as well as a professional finish and come in a range of weights and thicknesses; usually off-white or cream in color. You will need to join widths for wide drapes; in this case, overlap the long edges and herringbone-stitch them together (see page 178). The thickest type of interlining is bump, which resembles a fleecy blanket. Domette, a baize or coarse flannel, is a brushed cotton and a more commonly used alternative. A thinner, bonded synthetic-fiber interlining is suitable for use with lightweight textiles and fabrics made of synthetic fibers.

Batting or wadding is used to pad fabric. It is used to add bulk to hems or leading edges, to soften cornices or pelmets or with quilted items. It is usually off-white or gray in color and made from natural fibers; some synthetic types are available. A special heavy flock batting or wadding is useful for upholstery projects, such as softening headboards. Batting or wadding comes in three weights, light (2 oz/50 gm), medium (4 oz/100 gm) and heavy (8 oz/ 200 gm) and several widths. If it has to be joined, pull the edge of one sheet slightly over the other and herringbone-stitch together (see page 178). Several layers can also be used and should be similarly joined.

Sewing by Hand

Even though many modern sewing machines can produce an array of stitches there are times when hand sewing is necessary. For instance, before machining a seam you should baste or tack by hand to hold the fabric firmly in position; always remove basting stitches after machining. And often the only way to achieve a really neat finish is to sew by hand. The following hand stitches will come in useful when making all sorts of soft furnishing projects.

Running Stitch

Running stitch consists of small, neat stitches of equal length which are made on both sides of the fabric. Use for simple sewing and to gather fabric. To pull running stitches into a gather: begin on the right side of the fabric and either wind plenty of thread around a pin at the starting point to hold it. Make a line of stitches, passing the needle through from back to front of the work and finish by winding the thread around a second pin. Pull the threads by applying even pressure from each end to gather the fabric.

Basting or tacking is sewn in a similar way, but with longer stitches on the working side and smaller ones on the reverse side.

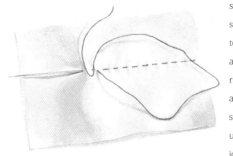

Use a contrasting colored thread so that the basting is easily visible for removal after the main stitching is completed.

Back Stitch

Back stitch is a short, strong stitch which may be used instead of machining on seams or for small, difficult areas. Two or three back stitches sewn on top of each other are useful for finishing thread ends securely when using other hand stitches. Take a stitch backward and insert the needle at the end of the previous stitch and bring the needle out an equal distance in front of the thread. Repeat back and forth until you have completed a line of firm stitching.

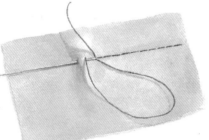

Ladder Stitch

Ladder stitch is useful when you need to match the pattern on the fabric exactly across a seam. Work on the right side of the fabric. On small areas this stitch may be used as final stitching; on larger areas it is a useful basting stitch before sewing a flat seam. Press the seam allowance turning down along one edge to the wrong side, place over the seam allowance on top of the matching piece on the right side, making sure that the pattern is aligned accurately. Pin at right angles to the seam. Insert the needle inside the fold of the upper layer and take a small stitch across the join through the under layer.

Slip Stitch

Slip stitch holds two folded edges of fabric together, for example on mitered corners or to attach trimmings. Work on the right side of the fabric, from right to left. Fold and press the turning to the wrong side of the fabric. Place the two folded edges parallel to each other. Slip the needle inside the fold on one edge and secure the thread with a couple of back stitches on top of each other. Take a small stitch inside the folded edge, sliding the needle along inside the fold for ¼in/0.75 cm. Bring the needle out of the fold and insert it into the other piece of fabric exactly opposite

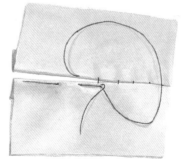

the point where the needle emerged. Catch a couple of threads from the opposite piece of fabric, so joining the two pieces together. Make sure that the fabric does not pucker.

Hemming Stitch

Hemming stitch holds a folded edge to flat fabric. Hand hemming produces a much neater finish that hemming by machine. Work on the wrong side of the fabric; with the folded edge facing toward you, point the needle diagonally from right to left. Pick up just a couple of threads from the flat piece of fabric. Bring the needle under the folded edge and up through the two layers of fabric. Repeat all along the hem. If the fabric is very heavy, turning under twice for a double hem may be too bulky. In this case, turn under once only and neaten the raw edge by adding straight binding to hide the raw edge or use herringbone stitch (see below).

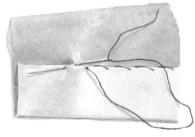

Herringbone Stitch

Herringbone or catch stitch is a flat stitch used instead of hemming on a raw edge. It is useful for bulky or heavy fabrics and curved hems and employed to join overlapping edges of batting or wadding. Work on the wrong side of the fabric from left to right. With the needle pointing right to left take a horizontal stitch through the flat layer of fabric, picking up just a couple of threads. Move the needle to the right and take a diagonal stitch again, right to left, through the folded edge of the fabric. Continue working the thread diagonally from right to left, making cross stitches across the hem edge.

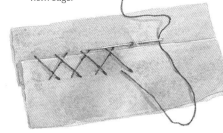

Blanket Stitch

Blanket stitch is worked over a straight raw or folded edge to neaten it. It is also used as decoration, particularly in appliqué work; use a contrasting color thread for a strong visual impact. Work with the right side of the fabric facing you. Fasten the working thread just under the fabric edge and insert the needle the desired distance at right angles to the edge. Take a stitch through the fabric, looping the working thread behind the needle before pulling it through to form a loop on the edge of the fabric.

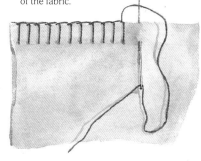

Buttonhole Stitch

Buttonhole stitch is similar to blanket stitch but the stitches are worked much more closely together to form a firm edge. It is used on the cut edges forming the opening of a buttonhole, to prevent the fabric from fraying and for stitching hooks and eyes and fasteners

firmly in place. Use heavier thread such as linen or silk for extra strength. (You can also work buttonholes by machine if you have the correct attachment.)

Work in the opposite direction to blanket stitch and insert the needle through the fabric the desired distance from the edge. Twist the working thread around the point of the needle. Pull this through so that the loop created with the thread forms a knot at the cut edge of the fabric. When you reach the corner of a buttonhole make a "bar" of stitches close together in a fan shape in order to prevent the buttonhole from splitting.

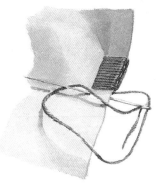

The usual method of making a buttonhole is by measuring and marking the position and length of the hole first on the fabric. With a single layer of fabric cut the slit for the hole so that it runs in the direction of the strain. However, it is more common to make buttonholes in a double layer of fabric. In this case, make two rows of basting or tacking stitches parallel to each other on each side of the slit mark to hold the layers of fabric together while you work the buttonhole. Cut a slit in between the rows of basting and proceed as before.

Sewing by Machine

A simple flat seam is the most commonly used seam in home sewing – it should be unobtrusive with no lines of stitching showing on the right side of the fabric. Before you begin any type of machine seaming, check that the grain of the fabric is straight by pulling a thread across the width. This is particularly important when using patterned fabric for making drapes as the design is sometimes printed slightly askew and you may have problems lining up the pattern in relation to the window. If it is not straight return the fabric to the supplier before cutting out. With many fabrics it is wise to remove the selvages before seaming as they may pucker and spoil the look of the seam. As an alternative, you can notch the selvage every few inches or centimetres once the seam is made, to prevent puckering.

Always stitch down the length of a seam, from top to bottom. If you are using a pile fabric like velvet make sure that the nap (the direction in which the pile lies) runs the same way on both sides of the seam or the join will be obvious. With a very heavy pile, if the fibers get caught in the seam, trim the pile within the seam allowance before stitching and ease any caught pile out of the seam with the point of a pin or a needle. If working with fine fabrics such as nets, sheers, muslin or voile use a fine-gauge needle and a suitable thread (see page 176). The layers of such fabrics tend to slip – this can also happen with silky fabrics and satin – so place strips of tissue paper in between the two layers and sew through the paper. If the fabric is likely to catch in the needle – this can occur with textured voiles – use tissue paper under the

foot of the sewing machine, in between it and the fabric. Tear away the paper after the seam is made and pick out any small scraps carefully with the point of a pin or a needle.

To eliminate unnecessary bulk from seams, trim the seam allowance close to the stitching line after machining. Do not do this on fabric which is likely to fray or the cloth may work itself loose from the seam. If you do not intend to press the seam open, but press it to one side, for example where piping is to run alongside it, cut only one seam allowance close to the stitching line to give a smoother effect on the right side; this is known as grading.

Flat Seam

To make a flat seam, first pin two pieces of fabric, matching any pattern, right sides together. Place the pins at right angles to the raw edges and space them at regular intervals down the line of the seam. Next baste or tack (see page 178) down the seamline at least ½ in/1.25 cm in from the open edge, removing the pins as you go. Machine alongside, but not over, the basting line. (If you are sewing by hand use back stitch, see page 178.) Secure the seam at both ends with a few reverse stitches. Remove the basting stitches and press the seam from the wrong side of the fabric to blend the stitches into the fabric. Open the seam flat and press the seam allowance down to either side, unless you want to neaten it first or you want the bulk of the seam to lie in one direction.

Once the flat seam is sewn and trimmed it may require neatening. The simplest way to do this is to machine a row of zigzag stitches along the raw edge of the fabric. If the fabric is not liable to fray, pinking with pinking shears

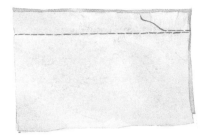

is a quick and easy solution. Fine fabrics can be turned under in a narrow fold and hemmed by hand (see page 178). If the fabric is bulky, you can bind the edges with straight seam binding.

Overlocking

Overlocking is a useful technique and encloses the raw edges of a seam to hide fraying. To overlock a flat seam: trim the top seam allowance to approximately ⅛ in/3 mm. Turn the edge of the other seam allowance under ⅛ in/3 mm and press. Turn again and place the folded edge along the flat seamline, to enclose the raw edge of the top seam allowance. Press again and hand hem (see page 178) the fold to the fabric as close to the seam line as possible.

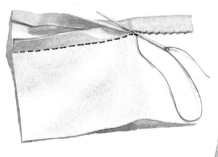

French Seam

If you require a totally enclosed finish with no lines of stitching showing on the right side of the fabric use a French seam. This is a very hard-wearing seam and is often used for pillowcases, laundry bags and loose covers. It is also useful for joining sheer fabrics when the seam will not be concealed by a lining. With wrong sides together and raw edges aligned, stitch a flat seam approximately ¼ in/0.75 cm in from the open edge and trim the seam allowances slightly to reduce the bulk. Press. Turn the fabric back on itself so the right sides are facing and the seam lies on the fold. Baste the two layers together about ½ in/1.25 cm below the seam line. Machine a second seam parallel to the first just above the basting line to enclose the raw edges. Remove the basting stitches. Press and turn the seam to the wrong side and the fabric right side out.

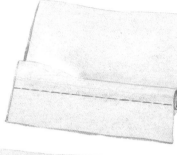

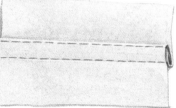

Flat Fell Seam

The flat fell seam gives a flat finish but two parallel rows of stitching will show on the right side of the fabric. It is used for joining raw edges for items such as bedspreads and tablecloths when a strong, hard-wearing seam with well-enclosed allowances is required. With the two pieces of fabric wrong sides together and raw edges aligned, stitch a flat seam approximately ½ in/1.25 cm in from the open edge. Press both seam allowances to one side. Trim the underneath seam allowance to approximately ⅛ in/3 mm. Turn ¼ in/6 mm of the upper seam allowance over the trimmed seam allowance, see the top illustration, above. Machine the top seam allowance to the fabric close to the edge of the fold, parallel to the first seam, so that the trimmed seam allowance is enclosed in the fold, see the lower illustration, above. Press.

How to Neaten Corners

When joining two flat pieces of fabric to make a right-angled corner, for example on a pillow or cushion, machine stitch straight into the corner and ensure that the needle is in the fabric when it reaches the corner; lift the foot and turn the fabric through 90° and continue stitching along the next side of the angle. Trim the corner by cutting across it at an angle to remove any surplus fabric for a neat finish, see below. If the corner is sharper than a right-angle, machine one, two or three stitches across the point , depending on the thickness of the fabric, and trim the corner across at an angle, see below. If you are machining a curved seam, perhaps for a rounded corner on a bedcover or a circular pillow or cushion or to make a bolster with rounded ends, snip notches at intervals along the curved edges in order to achieve a flat finish.

Mitering Corners

When two edges meet and need hemming you must miter the corner, see opposite. With the fabric wrong side up, turn in about ¼ in/0.75 cm along each edge and press. Fold along the hemlines. Press and unfold the hems. Fold in the corner so the diagonal fold aligns with the straight fold lines of the hem. Trim off the surplus triangle of fabric, leaving a ¼ in/0.75 cm seam allowance. Turn in one hem along the hemline crease. Press and pin. Turn in the other hem along the hemline crease to form a neat corner. Pin and hem stitch (see page 178). Slipstitch (see page 178) along the diagonal at the corner to secure.

Binding and Piping

Binding and piping add a neat finish and a professional look to all kinds of soft furnishings. They can be made from matching or contrasting fabric and add extra detail and help to outline or define the shape of an item. As piping and bias binding are cut on the cross some spectacular results can be achieved using striped or checked fabric. Bias and straight binding can be purchased ready-made but these are usually narrow in width and light in weight and so are more suitable for edging smaller items. Straight binding is useful for neatening hems.

Piping is made by covering a purchased piping cord with bias strips of fabric which is stitched into a flat seam (see page 179) to give a tailored finish. The cord is available in different thicknesses, so choose the size according to the scale of the item you wish to pipe. Shrink cotton cord carefully before use or It will cause the piping to pucker during washing. Do this by boiling the cord in a clean water for five minutes and allow to dry thoroughly before use. Always choose a fabric for binding or piping which is similar in type and weight to the main fabric. Make sure that it is shrink-resistant and color-fast so that it does not bunch or bleed and discolor the main fabric.

For binding and covering piping cord you need bias strips of fabric, this is more flexible and has more "give" in it. To find the true bias of a piece of fabric, fold a straight raw edge back parallel to the selvage to form a triangle of fabric – the base of the triangle is the true bias and is called the bias line. Mark out strips parallel to the bias line with a long ruler and tailor's chalk or a marker pen and

cut them out, according to the width you require. The most usual width is 1 ½ in/3.75 cm. To make the bias binding, join the strip to give a continuous length. To do this, place two strips together at right angles to each other with right sides facing; this will form a triangle. Pin and machine firmly across the width, leaving a ¼ in/0.75 cm seam allowance. Open out flat and press. Trim the corners to lie flat with the bias strip.

To cover piping cord, work out the length of piping required and join enough bias strips together to cover the cord. The bias binding must be wide enough to cover the cord and leave a ½ in/1.25 cm seam allowance

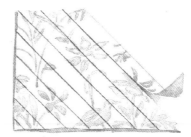

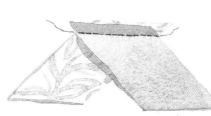

on both sides. Press the bias binding strip flat and place it right side down. Position the piping cord in the middle and wrap the binding with wrong sides facing to enclose the cord. Baste close to the cord but do not catch it. Machine stitch using a piping or zipper foot if you have one, or use firm back stitch (see page 178) if you are sewing by hand. Remove the basting stitches. If you have to join the cord, unravel two ends of cord and trim the

strands to varying lengths. Overlap the ends of the strands by about 1 in/2.5 cm and intertwine the strands so that they mesh to make a smooth join. Wrap the binding around the cord and stitch as before.

When you have covered the piping cord it is ready to sew into the main seam. Place the panel of main fabric wrong side down and lay the piping on top of it so that the raw edges of the binding face outward and align with the raw edge of the seam allowance of the main fabric. Baste together. Place the second panel of main fabric right side down over the top with the raw edges aligning and baste. Use a piping or zipper foot to machine the four layers together along the seamline or back stitch by hand (see page 178). Remove the basting. When you turn the fabric right side out the piping neatly edges the seam.

You can neaten a raw edge with bias binding by hand or by machine. Ready-made bias binding has pre-folded edges.

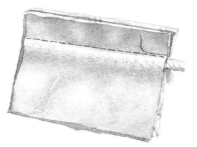

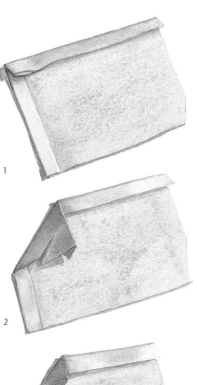

1

2

3

4

To miter a corner: turn in the edges (1). Fold along the hemlines and fold in the corner (2). Fold in the hem to form a diagonal (3). Fold in the second hem to form a diagonal and finish the corner with slipstitch (4).

If you are making your own bias binding from bias strips turn in a narrow edge to the wrong side along both long edges and press for a neat edge. To sew by hand, open one folded edge of the binding strip. Match this to the raw edge of the fabric to be bound placing the right sides together. Pin and back stitch (see page 178) together down the fold line of the binding, as shown above. Refold the binding and turn over onto the wrong side of the fabric to be bound, enclosing the raw edge. Pin in place and slip stitch (see page 178) the second folded edge of the binding to the fabric following the first line of stitching.

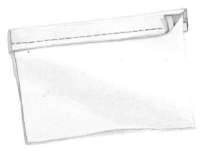

To neaten a raw edge with binding by machine, fold the binding down the middle and place wrong side down over the raw edge of the fabric to be bound. Press, baste and machine stitch through the fabric and both folds of the binding close to the edge of the binding. Remove the basting stitches.

Measuring Up Windows

For accurate measuring use a good-quality tape measure and a steel ruler or a wooden yard or metre stick; an old fabric tape measure may have stretched through use, so it may be less accurate. Refer to the illustration on page 183 for how to take essential measurements and note them all down on a sketch of your window. When purchasing fabric take the annotated sketch with you, this will help the retailer to advise you on correct quantities. It does help to have someone to assist you when measuring, to hold one end of the ruler and to double-check the measurements. You can measure in imperial or metric, depending on personal preference, although in Europe fabric is usually sold by the metre and shades or blinds are often quoted in metric sizes.

Drapes or Curtains

For measuring up drapes or curtains it is preferable to have the track or pole already in position, or to know at least how wide you want it and where exactly you plan to site it. The two measurements required for calculating fabric quantity are the width and the drop. For the width measurement: when using a track the complete track length should be measured and at least 4 in/10 cm added to each side for the returns. (Each return allows the drape to lie flush against the wall and hides the screws and fittings that support the track system.) For a pair of drapes, add an additional 3 in/7.5 cm for the overlap in the middle. If the drapes are to hang from a pole measure the pole length excluding the finials. The drop measurement depends on the type and style of heading used and whether the drapes are to hang from a pole or a track.

Decide whether the heading should hang level with, just above or just below the pole or track and calculate accordingly. Measure the drop from the top of the track, pole or window frame to the sill; then measure to the floor. Take these measurements as an extra check, even if you know you are going to have a floor-length or sill-length treatment, or if you plan to have the fabric bunching on the floor. Drapes that flap midway between the sill and floor look untidy, but sometimes, if there is a radiator under the window which does not quite come up to sill height, you may want to finish the drapes to line up with the top of the radiator, so take this measurement from the top of the track to the top of the radiator. Multiply the number of widths of fabric by the total drop of both drapes to give you the amount of fabric required.

The amount of wallspace available will affect your choice of window treatment so include the wallspace in your original measurements. Drapes need space to stack back against the wall or they will block out light from the window. If no wallspace is available a shade or blind can be the solution. If there is wallspace on one side only then a single drape caught to one side is appropriate. For good-quality drapery returns are essential as they will block out light that would otherwise escape between the drape and the wall or window. Also, when taking initial measurements consider the flooring. If this is not yet installed, consider that a thick carpet or raised flooring can alter measurements considerably. Take final measurements after the floor has been laid. Other obstructions such as pipes, radiators and outlets or sockets can spoil a treatment. Make sure that you check for these when measuring.

When measuring up drapes allowances are needed for hems and turnings. It is always wise to have a fairly deep hem – for example 5-8 in/15-20 cm – which can be weighted to make the drapes hang better. A generous hem will also allow for any shrinkage, due to condensation or in cleaning. Allow a minimum of 2 in/5 cm for the turn-over at the top. Add these allowances to the drop.

Most furnishing fabrics are woven in one of the following widths: 48 in/122 cm, 54 in/137 cm or 60 in/160 cm. So, with the particular heading in mind, calculate how many widths of fabric, when joined together, will give a satisfactory fulness to the drapes. When measuring up for a patterned fabric check the repeat measurements on the manufacturer's label, or measure this for yourself. The most common repeats occur 6 in/16 cm, 12 in/23 cm or 25 in/64 cm apart. When joining two widths of a patterned fabric the pattern must be matched up. This is achieved by dividing the cut drop measurement by the pattern repeat measurement and rounding it up to a whole number of repeats. Each cut drop must be made up of complete patterns. Each width cut will now be identical in pattern so the widths will match when they are joined together. The hem is an important part of the drape, so it is a good idea to choose which part of the fabric will fall at the bottom. In general, it is the pattern that will decide the hem line and it is preferable to have a row of whole motifs in the design at the bottom edge rather than a row of incomplete ones. To ensure that you can choose which part of the pattern will fall at the bottom, buy one extra pattern repeat of fabric. See the illustration opposite for how to measure up a window for drapes.

Shades or Blinds

Depending on the style of the shade or blind, measuring has to allow for the required method of fixing. Use a wooden ruler or metal tape for measuring the width and drop of the window area to be covered by the finished shade or blind. If the window is deeply recessed and has a wide reveal it is usual to position the shade or blind as close to the glass as possible. A Roman shade or blind is usually fixed on a wooden batten screwed into the underside of the top reveal. For the drop, measure from the top of the batten position to the sill and add at least 4 in/10 cm for turning at the top and hemming at the bottom. (On a window frame which is not recessed, the batten will have to be mounted on supports above the window, so increasing the drop.) For the width, measure from one side of the reveal to the other and add an extra 2 in/5 cm for side hems. For width measurements the side hems are not necessary if the fabric is pre-stiffened and will not fray.

Austrian or festoon shades or blinds are gathered along a heading tape which is fixed to the window by means of a special track, perhaps mounted on a batten, which fits inside the reveal, making it easy to remove the whole for washing. For Austrian shades or blinds, measure the drop from the top of the track to the sill and add approximately 3 in/7.5 cm for turning at the top and hemming at the bottom. The width is dictated by the type of heading tape and the length of the track used; make an allowance for side hems and joins in the fabric if necessary and also allow for pattern matching. For a festoon shade or blind double the drop measurement for a ruched effect and triple it for a really full finish; the width is calculated as for Austrian

shades or blinds. For a roller shade or blind add approximately 1 in/2.5 cm to the width for side hems and a minimum 12 in/30 cm to the drop for a lath channel at the bottom and attachment to the roller at the top.

If the window is not recessed, the shade or blind will have to be mounted on the window frame if possible, or just outside it; so you should take the measurements accordingly. If there is no suitable flat part, the wood batten or roller for a roller shade or blind will have to be mounted on the wall above the frame. The wood batten, mounted track or roller may be screwed to two or more small pieces of wood in order to project far enough beyond the window to pull down easily and clear the frame. See the illustration below right for how to measure up a window for a shade or blind.

How to measure up a window

Take note of all the following measurements when planning drapes or curtains and shades or blinds.

1	Length of drape fixture
2	Stack back (extension of fixture beyond the window)
3	Drop from fixture to sill
4	Drop from fixture to radiator
5	Drop from fixture to floor
6	Distance from fixture to ceiling
7	Distance from fixture to top of window
8	Height or depth of window (with no recess)
9	Height or depth of window (inside recess)
10	Width of window (with no recess)
11	Width of window (inside recess)

Top Treatments

The positioning of the track, pole or cornice or pelmet board is crucial to the success of a window treatment. When measuring up, you should not only measure the actual window but also take the measurement from the top of the window architrave to the molding or cornice or the ceiling itself to see how much headroom you have. Also measure the height of the top third of the window to see how much light you would lose with a cornice or pelmet. If you would lose a lot of light and there is little or no headroom then you should consider a different treatment.

Hard cornices or pelmets are fixed by means of a board; soft valances are fixed by means of a double track. Some cornices or pelmets are formed from rigid material like wood or hardboard, but others are made from stiffened fabric. The cornice or pelmet board has to be fixed at the top of the window in order to conceal the track. It is usually positioned about 2-3½ in/5-8 cm above the top of the window frame and projects at least 2 in/5 cm either side of the track to allow for end-stops and drape fulness. The cornice or pelmet width is determined by the size of the board and the depth depends entirely on the height of the window, and whether you want to make the whole treatment look taller or shorter; you can work out a suitable shape and depth by using a template.

For valances, the fabric quantity has to be calculated allowing for adequate fulness which is partly dependent on the type of heading. You will also need to work out the pattern repeat if the fabric has a design, as the pattern must join across the width.

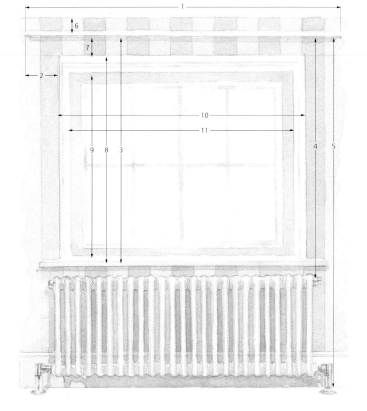

GLOSSARY

Accent color Small amounts of color, usually contrasting, introduced into a scheme to add interest or balance.

Acetate Also called Rayon or viscose; a man-made fiber made from cellulose (wood pulp) and spun like a regular fiber.

Advancing color The warm colors of the spectrum which appear to come toward you, creating an enclosing impression.

American cloth Type of oil cloth with a shiny surface, used for wipe-able tablecloths, drawer lining; in its thicker form used as a flooring.

Antimacassar Protective fabric covering for chair or sofa back to prevent soiling the base material – originally to protect against macassar oil worn by Victorian men on their hair.

Appliqué Literally applying a second layer of fabric onto a base cloth by decorative stitching or sticking in place to create a pattern.

Architrave The wooden molding surrounding a door or window.

Arts and Crafts A movement led by William Morris in the late 19th century dedicated to bringing back into the home simple design and high standards of craftsmanship.

Art Deco A style of design fashionable in 1920-30, characterized by solid rectilinear shapes and geometric and stylized motifs; in its purest form it relies on expensive, exotic materials.

Art Nouveau A decorative style at the turn of the century with emphasis on sinuous flowing lines.

Austrian shade or blind Also called festoons; a softly ruched fabric sheer or blind originally made in a sheer fabric.

Baize Lightweight felted wool cloth, traditionally green, generally used as a lining for drawers, doors, billard tables etc.

Basting thread Also called tacking thread; a method of loosely stitching fabric together before machine or hand stitching; a cotton thread is usual; choose a contrasting color to show up against the main fabric.

Batik Fabric dyeing technique; melted wax is painted onto cloth, usually cotton, before dyeing – when removed it leaves a characteristic smudged pattern.

Batting See wadding.

Bay window An angled projection of a house wall fitted with windows (normally on the front of the house); usually consists of three separate windows; may extend through several storeys forming a bay on each floor.

Beadwork Fabric patterned with sewn-on beads; may incorporate other embroidery highlighted with beads – used for pelmets, lambrequins, hems, borders etc.

Bed drapes or curtains Fabric drapes positioned above a bed, or used to dress a four poster.

Bias binding or strip Also called crossway strip; a strip of cloth cut diagonally from selvedge to selvedge to give stretch to the strip, for edging or to enclose piping cord.

Blend Also called union; a term given to a mixture of fibers in one cloth to improve handle and wear – a linen/cotton union is popular for upholstery.

Block-printing Hand printing using carved wooden blocks to transfer the dye to fabric or paper – the major form of printing until mid-18th century.

Boss Also called hold backs; a metal or wooden shape fixed to a wall to hold back drapes to let in more light, or used to hold back over-bed drapes.

Bouclé Fabric with curled or looped surface, usually of heavier weight, suitable for upholstery.

Bow window Similar to a bay window but the projection is curved.

Box pleat Flat, symmetrical pleat formed by folding the fabric to the back of each side of the pleat.

Braid A type of woven ribbon used to edge shades or blinds; trim pillows or cushions and drapes; cover joins in fabric and disguise tacks in upholstery.

Brocade A rich Jacquard-woven fabric with a matte backround and all-over raised design in a silky texture traditionally made of silk or cotton, sometimes with gold or silver added - nowadays can be made from any fiber.

Brocatelle Cloth similar to damask, usually self-colored with a raised satin or twill pattern on plain or satin ground, containing a double warp.

Broderie Anglaise A cotton fabric available in white or pastel colors with a lacy embroidered pattern; it is usually cut out; and frequently sold as a frill for trimming pillowcases, towels, cushions etc.

Buckram Coarse fabric of cotton or jute stiffened with size used to line hand-made drape headings; stiffen cornices or pelmets and tie-backs etc.

Bullion fringe A type of long silky fringe used to trim drapes.

Bump Also called interlining; fibrous cotton wadding used to interline drapes to give bulk.

Burlap Also called hessian; a strong, coarsely-woven fabric usually made from jute or hemp yarn – the rougher natural form is used in upholstery; to protect furniture in transport etc; dyed it is used for wallcovering – this is more successful when paper-backed.

Café curtain A "half curtain", slotted onto a pole, which is usually kept closed across the window to prevent passers by from seeing in.

Calendering Process of passing cloth between heavy rollers under friction to impart sheen to the surface.

Calico Plain woven cotton fabric slightly heavier and coarser than muslin – usually natural but can be bleached white.

Cambric Fine, firm cotton that is plain woven; often calendered and stiffened slightly; used for inner covers of pillows and duvets.

Candlewick Plain fabric with coarse cotton tufts which form a texture or pattern on the surface; used mainly for bedspreads.

Canvas Also called duck; a firm, strong, heavy fabric traditionally woven from linen, cotton or nowadays from synthetic fibres; the method of weaving renders it almost waterproof; used for ship's sails, awnings, tents etc; can be dyed or unbleached and comes in a variety of weights.

Casement window Vertically hinged window framed in timber or metal, opening inward or outward like a door.

Casing Also called cased heading; a simple double-hemmed top to drapes through which a rod or narrow pole may be slotted.

Ceiling rose Also called a centerpiece; a circular ornament placed in the middle of a ceiling, from which a light fitting may be suspended; originally made from carved wood or plaster.

Chair rail Also called a dado rail; a wooden or plaster molding fixed about 3ft/90cm from the floor; originally devised to prevent the backs of chairs from damaging fabric-hung walls; it provides a convenient boundary between different wall treatments.

Chaise longue A type of sofa or couch with one arm higher than the other, which is used for reclining.

Cheesecloth Another name for muslin; a soft, fine, light cotton or cotton mix fabric which drapes well and allows light to filter through; Swiss muslin is embroidered and used for accessories.

Chenille Yarn or fabric with a thick, soft velvety pile; originally made from wool or cotton it can now also be synthetic; it was popular in the 19th century as door and window drapes to keep out drafts.

Chesterfield A button-backed sofa, frequently upholstered in leather.

Chiné Also called warp print or shadow tissue; a patterned fabric with a blurred printed design showing on both sides, achieved by printing the parallel warp yarns before weaving with a plain weft; nowadays the look is sometimes mimicked by printing.

Chinoiserie The use of Oriental motifs in Western interior decoration and furnishing which became popular in the 18th century – it extended to furniture including that made by Chippendale called "Chinese Chippendale".

Chintz A cotton fabric traditionally printed with colorful patterns of flowers, fruits and birds made popular in the 18th century; nowadays used to describe a glazed fabric, which is resin-finished.

Complementary colors Contrasting or "opposite" colors; when used together in a room they create a stimulating effect.

Contrast binding Strips of contrasting fabric of various widths sewn on the edges of drapes, shades or blinds, valances, cornices or pelmets, tie-backs etc.

Corduroy Firm cloth with charac-teristic evenly-spaced ribbed pile running down the length of the fabric; originally made of cotton, but now it can be made in almost any fiber.

Cornice Fibrous plaster or wooden decorative molding that runs along the top of a wall or around the edge of a ceiling, usually disguising the join between the two. It can also be used to describe a type of preformed pelmet above a window, made usually of wood or stiffened fabric.

Corona A structure or bracket usually shaped like a crown, fixed to the wall above a bed, throne or sofa and used to suspend draperies.

Cotton Natural fiber which comes from the boll of the cotton plant; it is spun and woven into fabric with endless uses.

Coving Similar to a cornice but simpler in style.

Cretonne Printed furnishing cotton similar to chintz but heavier and with-out a glaze, available also in a twill.

Crewelwork Thin worcested yarn generally embroidered in chain stitch or herringbone stitch onto cotton, linen or wool; originally from India, the designs depicted the tree of life, flowers and foliage; used as early English and American bed hangings.

Crossway strip See bias.

Crushed velvet Velvet pile cloth, processed to flatten the pile so that the tufts then lie in different directions, creating an interesting texture.

Cut drop Finished length of the drapes or curtain which includes a turning allowance for the heading at the top and the hem at the bottom.

Dado Lower area of wall below the dado (or chair) rail and base or skirting board. Traditionally wood panelled or covered with heavily-textured wallcovering or tiled to make a practical surface to withstand knocks.

Damask Firm self-patterned fabric made on a jacquard loom from cotton, linen, silk or a combination of fibers; traditionally used for fine table linens.

Decorator or furnishing cotton Natural yarn woven into many qualities, some durable enough for upholstery; others as light-weight voiles.

Denim Strongly-woven hard-wearing fabric originally used for the characteristic blue working overalls; now used for upholstery and covers as well as jeans and other clothing.

Dobby cloth Fabric produced on a dobby loom which creates small, regularly repeated simple woven designs, sometimes textured.

Domette A baize or coarse flannel in which the warp is cotton and the filling woollen; used to interline drapes.

Door jamb The top and sides of the frame against which a door closes.

Dormer window A window set in, and projecting from a sloping roof, to provide light in a loft or attic room.

Double-cloth Strong, reversible fabric consisting of two separate cloths which each have their own warp and weft, which are interwoven.

Double-hung window Also called a sash window; it slides open vertically.

Draw rod A rod inserted into the heading to open and close drapes.

Dress drapes Also called show drapes; they do not close across the window, but which are merely hung for effect.

Duck See canvas.

Dupion Originally a fabric made from irregular thicknesses of silk to create a slubby texture; now can be made from other fibers.

Duplex print Fabric printed on two sides to give a reversible pattern.

Dust ruffle See valance.

Embossed fabric Fabric with a textured, raised and indented pattern which is created by engraved, heated rollers – can be used on many different fabrics, but embossed velvet is one of the most common.

End stop A plastic, metal or other fixing on the end of the track to prevent the drapes from sliding off.

Espagnole bolts Opening, closing or locking device, used on centrally-opening French windows or doors.

Eyelet Small metal ring inserted into fabric creating a bound hole through which ties, cords, laces, string etc. can be inserted.

Face cloth Term used for the main fabric of a drape.

Face fitting Fixing shades or blinds or drapes outside a window recess.

Fanlight Window set above a door, traditionally semi-circular with evenly spaced glazing bars set in a fan-like pattern.

Fascia A rectangular board set vertically to cover a drape heading or shade or blind fixing.

Felt Unwoven cloth made from a mass of animal fibers, pounded together until shrunk and matted in a strong bond; does not fray when cut.

Finial The decorative end to a metal or wooden drape pole, used to prevent the hooks from slipping off the end.

Finished length Length from the top to the bottom of the finished drape.

Flame-retardant fabrics Fabrics which are inherently flameproof (such as wool), or treated to be fire resistant. Government guidelines apply to ensure safety.

Flannel Smooth woollen self-colored fabric, can have fine chalk stripes.

Flatweave Also called tapestry weave; a process of weaving where the weft threads are not carried the full width of the fabric, but woven as they are needed in the design; the weft completely covers the warp; the fabric is reversible.

Flemish heading A goblet heading in which the pleats are linked along their base by a hand-sewn cord.

Floorcloth Painted canvas used on a hard floor instead of carpet or rugs.

French pleat Also called a pinch pleat; a drape heading with hand-sewn triple pleats with a flat area between them.

Frieze The area of wall between the picture rail and cornice or coving and the ceiling.

Fustian Heavy-duty down-proof calico with a close ribbed or twill weave which is used as an initial cover for cushions, pillows, bolsters, eiderdowns etc.

Gaufrage See embossed fabrics.

Genoa velvet Velvet patterned during weaving, with a multi-colored pile and satin ground; originally hand-woven in Genoa.

Georgette Fine fabric with a crêpe texture which drapes well and is used for sheer curtains, bed drapes, table covers and Austrian shades or blinds.

Gimp A delicate woven braid trimming; often contains metallic thread.

Gingham Traditional checked fabric, usually in cotton, woven in white with one other color to create the characteristic checked pattern.

Glasscloth Also called a tea towel; traditionally a piece of striped linen, cut to size and hemmed, used for drying clean glasses; may now be made of cotton or other fibers.

Glazing bars Wooden or metal strip within a window frame, separating one pane of glass from another.

Goblet heading Drape heading with fat "goblet" shaped pleats; the tops of these tubes are filled with wadding or batting or contrasting fabric.

Half-tester A shallow rectangular canopy above a bed; drapes at either side create a three-dimensional effect.

Heading Top edge of a drape which is finished with tape, hooks, rings or other treatment, by which means the fabric is suspended from a track or pole.

Heading tape Gathering tape, purpose-made to create various heading styles.

Herringbone A twill weave achieved by alternating a diagonal pattern within the cloth; also a hand-stitching method used to neaten raw edges.

Hessian See burlap.

Hold backs See boss.

Hopsack Fabric woven to create a fairly loose basket-weave effect.

Hue A pure color.

Holland shade or blind Finely woven canvas used in the 18th and 19th centuries for roller shades or blinds to protect furnishings or carpets from the sun; always a natural color.

Ikat Fabric patterned by resist-dyeing; the yarns are bound tightly and dyed, then untied and rebound in a different place and redyed a different color. The yarn is then woven creating patterns with vaguely defined outlines.

Interlining Soft material sewn between a drape and its lining to add bulk, to improve handle, drape, hang and bulk; to act as insulation. See also bump, domette.

Inverted pleat Also called a kick pleat; an inverted pleat formed like a box pleat in reverse so the edges of the pleats meet to conceal the extra fabric. Frequently used at the corner of a bed, chair or sofa cover.

Italian stringing Also called reefing; a means of raising or opening drapes which have a fixed heading (which is kept permanently closed) by means of threading cord through small rings sewn to the back of the drape.

Jacquard Cloth woven on a Jacquard loom, which uses perforated cards to control the pattern, enabling elaborately figured reversible fabrics to be woven.

Jardinière drapes Sheer drapes, sometimes lace, which arch in the middle of the lower edge allowing part of the window or view to be revealed.

Jute Fibrous material from the stem of the corchorus plant processed to make a suitable strong yarn used in weaving burlap or hessian as backing for carpets etc.

Kapok Loose fibers from a tree used to form wadding or batting as a stuffing to fill pillows; padding in upholstery etc.

Kelim A pileless ethnic wool, cotton or silk rug woven by the tapestry technique, characterized by narrow slits between blocks of color, creating simple bold geomeric patterns.

Kick pleat See inverted pleat.

Knole sofa A form of sofa or couch evolved in the 17th century, and named after Knole House in Kent; the high upholstered back and sides are hinged and can be let down to form a day bed; when closed they are usually tied to the frame with attractive tassled ties.

Lace A fine openwork fabric created by knotting or twisting threads to form a pattern against a net-like background; usually in white or cream and traditionally made of cotton, although other fibers and colors are now used; available in edgings and already-gathered frills and ruffles.

Lambrequin A stiff, shaped surround to a window, which goes across the top, like a cornice or pelmet, but then continues down the sides.

Lawn A fine soft, smooth, lightweight, slightly sheer fabric usually made from cotton, but can be linen or polyester yarn; traditionally used for making fine-quality handkerchiefs.

Leaded lights Square or diamond-shaped panes of glass set in lead to form a window; originally a Tudor design, this enabled small pieces of glass to be used for widow glazing.

Leading edge The front edges of a pair of drapes which meet in the middle of the window when the drapes are closed.

Linen A strong cloth spun from flax, prone to creasing and shrinkage which is why it is often combined with another fiber into a blend or union.

Lining A secondary fabric hung at the back of drapes, or used to back other fabric to create extra strength and drapeability, prevent fading, keep out the light etc. A firmly-woven cotton sateen is the most usual, which comes in creams, beige and white and a range of colors; insulated and dim-out linings are also available.

Lintel Beam carrying the load over a door or window.

Linterfelt Another name for fibrous waste cotton bump, interlining, wadding.

Loose covers Also called slip covers; extra loose easy-care covers which can be slipped onto chairs, sofas or couches to protect them and give a change of seasonal scene.

Louvred shades or blinds Slatted shades or blinds with wide vertical slats which can be made of wood, metal, plastic or specially-woven fabric; can be used as room dividers as well as up at windows.

Madras cotton Brightly colored, inexpensive Indian fabric in various striped and checked designs, prone to fading. Madras can also be used to describe an open-weave, gauze-like fabric with a woven pattern, sometimes called sari fabric.

Matelasse Thick, double cloth with a quilted effect; it is woven by double sets of warp and weft threads, and interlined at regular intervals, joining the cloths and creating the quilted look.

Mattress ticking See ticking.

Mercerized cloth A cold, concentrated solution of caustic soda is applied to woven cotton, linen or cellulose fiber cloth to cause irreversible swelling of the fibers to impart lustre to the surface.

Metre or yard stick A metal or wooden stick marked with centimetres or inches used for measuring.

Moiré A variation of the calendering process, where specially engraved rollers are used to create a characteristic water-marked effect, often on taffeta cloth; eventually wears away with consistent cleaning or washing.

Monochromatic scheme A color scheme based on different values – strengths or weights – of one color.

Moquette Also called *epinglé*; a fabric woven like velvet by looping the warp yarn over wires which are then withdrawn to form loops. It is very firm and used for upholstery; the loops can be cut or left uncut.

Mullions Vertical bars of stone or wood dividing the glazing of a window.

Muslin Also called calico, but this is more firmly woven. It is a soft, very light fabric, plain-woven in loose fashion to make it semi-sheer but it can be woven in different weights – the firmest weave is called calico.

Nacré velvet Two-tone velvet woven with one color for the ground and another for the pile.

Nap The fibrous surface or pile of a fabric; it affects the way in which the cloth reflects light and its apparent color. Great care should be taken when cutting fabric with a nap to ensure, when the pieces are joined, that all the nap faces in the same direction, otherwise the join becomes obvious.

Net A fine, lightweight fabric originally made from cotton (now usually made from a synthetic fiber) used for drapes and sheers.

Opening light The opening part of a window.

Open-weave Another word for a coarsely woven sheer fabric.

Organdie Hard-wearing, finely woven thin cotton cloth which is semi-transparent and stiff; it can be used to create crisp pleated effects.

Ottoman Ribbed cloth, in which the alternate ribs, running from selvage are raised. Also a name for a box with padded lift-up top, traditionally used as seating or for bedlinen storage.

Paisley A printed or woven design with rich, curvilinear highly-stylized floral forms with a Mogul influence, derived from shawls imported from India and then produced in Paisley in Scotland.

Patio windows Sliding windows, usually metal-framed which permit easy access to a patio, porch or verandah.

Pelmet Also called a cornice; a shaped piece of material or fabric hung at the top of drapes to hide the track. It can be made from wood or stiffened fabric mounted onto a board.

Pencil pleat or heading A drape heading formed by a tape, which when drawn up creates a row of narrow, densely-packed folds.

Percale A fine-quality, plain woven cotton cloth which is now synonymous with superior bedlinens.

Petitpoint Close, hand-embroidered stitch, which is usually done in tapestry wool; it is mainly used for chair backs and other upholstery, rugs etc.

Picture rail A simple beading running around the walls of a room immediately below the frieze from which pictures can be suspended by means of hooks and wires.

Picture window A large, landscape-shaped window made from one flat piece of glass, with no glazing bars, to allow full enjoyment of a view.

Piece-dyed Cloth that is dyed after weaving.

Pile Fabric with tufts or loops formed on the face of the cloth.

Pinch pleat See French pleat.

Pinoleum Very narrow, thin wooden slats used to form shades or blinds.

Piping Neat edging to seams, pillows or cushions etc, created by covering piping cord with cloth and seaming together with the fabrics to be joined.

Piqué Ribbed woven cotton fabric similar to twill; slightly stiff in texture and frequently produced in white.

Plantation shutters Louvred internal shutters traditionally made from wood; a metal rod controls the opening and closing of the louvres.

Plissé shades or blinds Permenently-pleated shades or blinds made of paper, polyester or special insulating fiber; usually semi-opaque.

Plush Long pile fabric similar to velvet but with a longer, less dense pile lying in one direction; popular for table covers and door drapes in the 19th century.

Polyester A man-made fiber made from the by-products of petrol refining.

Poplin Plain weave cotton cloth with fine weft-way ribs.

Portière drape and rod A drape which hangs behind a door to completely cover it and keep out drafts; it has to be suspended from the special rod which rises and falls as the door opens.

Pre-corded track Drape track with an integral cording system for closing and opening the drapes.

Printed cloth Any cloth to which a colored design has been added by mechanical process eg roller, silk-screen.

Print room Method of patterning walls fashionable during the 18th century; prints were either cut out and stuck to the wall, or framed and hung in position, they were then joined by stuck-on or stencilled garlands, ribbons and bows; sometimes the effect was painted in *trompe l'oeil*.

Provençal print French country prints with brightly colored small motifs (scaled-down Paisley) and floral designs usually on cotton; also produced on oilcloth; originally hand-blocked; good for mix-and-match.

Push-through Controlled application of printed dyes so color permeates the cloth, the design shows on the reverse creating a Duplex print.

Rattan Thin, pliable leaves of a palm which are dried and woven into shades or blinds, matting etc.

Raw edge The cut edge of fabric, which often frays and needs neatening.

Raw silk Also called wild silk; natural fiber produced by the lavae of the silk worm, which is then spun and woven into a lustrous fabric; raw or wild silk is more irregular and yields a yarn with a slubby coarse texture.

Rayon See acetate, viscose.

Receding color A cool color which apears to go away from you, creating an impression of greater space in an interior.

Recess The window niche into which a window is fitted.

Recessed fitting Drape or shade or blind fixed within the recess of a window.

Reefed drapes See Italian Stringing.

Repeat The full length of a vertical design, taken from one point to the next point where it repeats itself exactly; accurate measuring is essential when making drapes or covers to allow for pattern matching when the fabric is seamed to the next width.

Rep Strong mono-colored ribbed cloth with ribs running from selvage; usually woven from cotton.

Return The flat outside edge of the drape or curtain that covers the return to the wall; the distance between the face of the track or pole to the wall or window casing.

Reveal The side walls of a window niche.

Roller shade or blind A simple shade or blind operated with a spring mechanism so that it rolls up neatly around the cylinder when raised.

Roller or cylinder printing Engraved metal rollers or cylinders are used to print a design on fabric; originally used to "print" engravings and then developed for wallpaper; finally adapted to fabric printing in 17th century.

Roman shade or blind A tailored shade or blind which forms lateral pleats when raised and is flat when closed.

Rosette A circular fabric "rose" which is used as a "finishing off" motif for drape headings, tie-backs, swags and tails etc. It can be knife-pleated, *choux* or bow style.

Rouleau fastening A fastening made with a rolled piece of fabric, originally silk.

Ruched shade or blind Also called a festoon shade or blind; it is gathered up into soft folds by means of tapes or rings and cords stitched to the back.

Sari Traditional dress worn by women in India; consists of a long, narrow piece of cloth.

Sarill A synthetic interlining which is fleecy without having the weight of bump.

Sash window Also called a double hung window; it is composed of two halves which slides up and down vertically to open on runners by means of sash cords.

Sateen Firmly woven fabric created by passing each weft thread over four warp threads, then under one, to produce a smooth lustrous look and feel; method of weaving used to produce drape lining fabric.

Satin Lustrous drapeable fabric made from silk, cotton or synthetic fibers produced in a similar fashion to sateen. It is closely woven to show much of the warp and produce a smooth, shiny face and a matte reverse side.

Scalloped heading or edging A heading or edging with deep, round cutouts; in the case of a heading the scallops slot onto a pole.

Seam allowance Extra fabric left on the narrow edge of a seam to allow for fabric fraying; this must be calculated and allowed for when buying fabric.

Seam ripper Metal device for unpicking seams and stitches.

Seersucker Characteristic "puckered" and flat cloth created by using a mixture of fibers – one of which will shrink creating a ruched effect; usually woven in cotton but other fibers can be used; can also be made by applying heat to synthetic fibers; designs are usually checks or stripes.

Selvage Firmly woven edge of woven fabric running parallel to the warp, down the length of the fabric. It may have the pattern repeat indicated on it, which helps with matching up. In some cases it should be trimmed or notched so that the work does not pucker when seamed.

Shade Also called a blind; name given to flat or ruched fabric covering a window, usually situated close to the glass, which pulls up horizontally or laterally. See also Austrian shade, roller, Roman etc.

Shantung Plain, woven fabric with a rich, slubby texture originally of silk, but now imitated in synthetic fibers; used for opulent furnishings.

Sheers Thin, translucent fabric such as lace, lawn, muslin, net, voile used to create a light-filtering window screen when privacy is required; may also be used in lavish bed draping or for dressing table "skirts".

Sheeting Fairly finely woven cotton or cotton blend fabric sold in wider-than-normal widths so it can be made up into sheets, duvet covers etc. It may be used as other furnishing cottons.

Shirring Method of drawing up fabric by means of tiny stitches which are then pulled up tightly to form gathers.

Shot taffeta Effect produced by using contrasting colors in warp and weft threads; the cloth changes appearance or color according to the way that light falls on it.

Show drapes See dress drapes.

Shutters Window coverings made of wood or metal; these can be internal, when they usually fit into a "box" each side of the window during the day, closing across close to the glass at night, or may be external; nowadays used as a security device.

Silk screen printing Process of printing similar to stencilling; the colorant or dye is forced through a prepared screen made of fine mesh.

Sill Horizontal beam or frame edge at the bottom of a door or window.

Skirt A name for a gathered table or dressing-table cover, or a frill which covers the feet of upholstered furniture.

Skirting board Also called a baseboard; narrow panel of wood fixed horizontally between the floor and wall of a room.

Slip cover See loose cover.

Slot heading Method of suspending drapes and bedhangings by means of the fabric itself; can be created by a casing, slots, loops or castellations at the top of the drape.

Slub Introduction of a slightly thicker thread at irregular intervals along the length of a finer one creates a "slubby" textured fabric; this is seen in naural fibers – linen, silk and in various synthetics and in weaves such as dupion, shantung and raw or wild silk.

Smocked heading Drape heading made of pencil pleats fixed together at regular intervals to create a honeycomb or smocked effect.

Soffit The "ceiling" of a recessed window.

Squab Flat, removable pillow or cushion pad which is used to soften wooden or metal chair seats, backs etc.

Swags and tails A decorative arrangement of fabric hung at the top of the drape; swags are draped in a generous horizontal scoop; tails hang so that they fall fluidly, or in firm triangular folds at the end of the swags.

Synthetic fibers A large group of fibers used alone or in blends or unions to create fabrics; mainly made by grouping chemicals as a by-product of petroleum. For instance, acrylic, nylon, polyester, Terylene, vinyl; or from cellulose, for example, acetate, Celanese, Rayon, viscose.

T-pins Special large pins used to hold heavy cloth to an upholstered item when cutting out covers.

Taffeta Plain, woven cloth with subtle ribs across the width creating a silky texture; the closer the ribs the stiffer the fabric.

Tails See swags and tails.

Tape-gathered heading Drape heading formed by specially woven tape which is sewn to the top of the drape; when cords are pulled up the heading is formed; can create many styles including French or pencil pleats.

Tapestry Heavy, woven fabric often of traditional pictorial design used for upholstery, hangings etc. Originally hand-embroidered or woven wall-hangings depicting heroic scenes; also decribes a method of weaving, see flat weave.

Tartan Traditional woollen cloth woven in two or more colors to create a checked design; individual tartan designs relate to specific family, place or regimental names in Scotland and Ireland.

Template A pattern, usually of card, plastic or other firm material which is used as a guide when cutting out fabric.

Tented ceiling Ceiling draped in fabric from a central point to imitate the inside of a tent.

Ticking Also called mattress ticking; heavy cotton twill fabric, usually in a herringbone texture, used for pillows, mattresses, bolsters, etc. It is closely woven to prevent penetration of fillings such as down, horsehair etc. Traditionally woven with fine stripe in black, blue, red on off-white.

Tint A pale value of a color created by adding white to a pure hue.

Toile A "pattern" cut in inexpensive fabric, usually calico, used to test an effect before the more expensive face cloth is cut out; can be used as a lining.

Toile de Jouy Traditional cotton print in one color on a natural or off-white ground, usually red, blue or sepia, depicting romantic pictorial scenes of rustic figures and foliage; originally made by engraved copper rollers at the Oberkampf factory at Jouy-en-Josas in the 18th century.

Tone A mid-tone value of a color created by adding gray to a pure hue.

Touch-and-close fastening Also called Velcro; double tape used for closing – one side of the tape is covered with nylon fuzz; the other side with tiny nylon hooks which catch together when the two surfaces are pressed together.

Towelling Thick, absorbent cut pile fabric woven from cotton which is generally made up into towels but also sold by the yard or metre. It can be used for upholsery, pillows or cushions and more. Terry towelling has uncut loops and can be more luxurious in handle.

Trompe l'oeil Literally "to deceive the eye"; a method of painting scenes, architectural features such as niches onto a flat wall – sometimes on canvas stretched onto battens – to create a three-dimensional effect, made popular during 17th and 18th century. This look can also be printed on fabric; painted on wood or plaster to make them look more exotic.

Turkey work Heavy, woven fabric or embroidery made by using knots to imitate the look of hand-woven rugs from the Near East; used for pillows or cushions, upholstery, hangings etc.

Tweed Cloth made with woollen yarns in a variety of weaves, textures and colors; adds warmth and comfort to a furnishing scheme in upholstery, bedcovers, throws, pillows etc.; does not drape very well for curtains.

Twill type of weave which produces a hard-wearing cloth with diagonal ribbed lines within the fabric; herringbone is produced by alternating the diagonal.

Union See blend.

Utrecht velvet Cut-pile fabric, traditionally mohair on linen, with a pattern created by crushing areas of pile using heated engraved rollers.

Valance Also called a dust ruffle; frill of fabric which can be used at the top of a drape to conceal the heading and track mechanism; around the hem of a loose or slip cover; and around the base of a bed to conceal it or the frame and legs.

Value The weight or strength of a color – sometimes called a tone.

Velcro See touch-and-close fastening.

Velour Heavy fabric with a thick warp-pile which lies in one direction giving a velvet-like finish.

Velvet Thick, soft, luxurious warp-pile fabric with a dense short pile produced either by lifting the warp threads over wires or metal strips and then cutting the loop formed; or by the face-to-face method of weaving, when two cloths are woven simultaneously facing each other and sliced apart as they come off the loom to produce two velvet-pile cloths; terry velvet has an uncut pile.

Velveteen Cotton velvet made with a short, thick weft pile rather than a warp-pile.

Viscose See acetate and synthetic fibers.

Voile Lightweight fabric which appears crisp and transluscent, it is for all kinds of soft furnishings, for example as sheer drapes or curtains, gathered shades or blinds; for draping dressing tables and beds. It can be woven from cotton, silk, synthetic fibers and may have a slight raised texture such as spots, dots, diamonds etc. incorporated for design interest.

Wadding Thick cotton or polyester padding which is soft and fibrous is available in various weights. Used for upholstery, to pad cornices or pelmets and for quilting.

Wainscot Simple wooden covering or lining of interior walls before more sophisticated panelling was introduced, usually to dado height; is also applied to a wood-clad dado or a deep baseboard or skirting.

Warp Also called ends; lengthwise threads on a loom threaded onto the loom under tension; weft threads are interlaced over and under them, by various methods (ie bobbin, shuttle or wires) to create a woven cloth.

Warp-faced Textile in which a large proportion of the warp threads are on the surface, hiding the weft.

Watered finish Method of producing a watered effect on cloth by using heated rollers, see moiré, tattefa.

Weft Also called picks or woof; the crosswise threads on a loom, are interlaced over and under the warp threads. It refers to the yarn woven across the width of the fabric through the lengthwise warp yarn.

Width Measurement across the fabric from selvage to selvage; standard widths are usually 36 in/120 cm; 48 in/137 cm; 60 in/150 cm. However, some fabrics such as sheeting are available in larger widths; widths have to be seamed together in order to make wide drapes, covers etc.

Window "furniture" Name given to metal attachments on windows such as bolts, handles, catches and stays.

Wool Natural fiber produced from the fleece of animals – usually sheep but can be goats, camels, etc.

Worsted Hard-wearing fabric woven with a closely twisted yarn made from combed wool. It has a hard, smooth and close-textured surface and no nap.

DIRECTORY

Fabric suppliers

In the UK:

Abbott & Boyd
88 Garlands Road
Redhill
Surrey RH1 6NZ

Andrew Martin
International Ltd
200 Walton Street
London SW3 2JL

Anna French Ltd
108 Shakespeare Road
London SE24 0QQ

Anta
Fearn by Tain
Ross'shire
Scotland IV20 1TL

Beaumont & Fletcher Ltd
134 Lots Road
London SW10 0RJ

Belinda Coote Tapestries
29 Holland Street
London W8 4NA

Bennett Silks
Crown Park Royal
Higher Hillgate
Stockport
Cheshire SK1 3HB

Bennison Fabrics
16 Holbein Place
London SW1W 8NL

Bernard Thorp & Co Ltd
6 Burnsall Street
London SW3 3SR

Brian Yates
Riverside Park
Caton Road
Lancaster LA1 3PE

Brooke London/Alton
Brooke
5 Sleaford Street
London SW8 5AB

Brunschwig & Fils
10 The Chambers
Chelsea Harbour Drive
London SW10 0XF

Busby & Busby
63 Salisbury Street
Blandford Forum
Dorset DT11 7PY

Celia Birtwell
71 Westbourne Park Road
London W2 5QH

Chase Erwin Ltd
22 Chelsea Garden Market
Chelsea Harbour
London SW10 0XE

Chelsea Textiles
39 Thurloe Square
London SW7 2SR

Colefax and Fowler
39 Brook Street
London W1Y 2JE

Cover-up of Kingsclere
9 Kingsclere Park
Kingsclere
Newbury
Berkshire RD15 8SW

D G Distribution
26 Old Church Street
London SW3 5BY

Danielle Ltd
33 Elystan Street
London SW3 3NT

Designers Guild
277 Kings Road
London SW3

Donghia
23 Chelsea Garden Market
Chelsea Harbour
London SW10 0XE

Dovedale Fabrics
13 Mount Road
Feltham
Middlesex TW13 6AR

Firifiss
PO Box 1464
Bournemouth
Dorset BH4 9QY

G P & J Baker
PO Box 30
West End Road
High Wycombe
Buckinghamshire
HP11 2QD

Gainsborough Silk Weaving Co Ltd
Alexandra Road
Chilton
Sudbury
Suffolk CO10 6XH

George Spencer Designs
4 West Halkin Street
London SW1X 8JA

Guy Evans Ltd
51A Cleveland Street
London W1P 5PQ

Henry Bertrand
108 Judd Street
London WC1H 9NT

Henry Newbery & Co Ltd
18 Newman Street
London W1P 4AB

Hill & Knowles Ltd
13 Mount Road
Feltham
Middlesex TW13 6AR

Hodsoll McKenzie
52 Pimlico Road
London SW1W 8LP

Ian Mankin
109 Regents Park Road
London NW1

Ian Sanderson (Textiles) Ltd
PO Box 148 Newbury
Berkshire
RG15 9DW

JAB
15-19 Cavendish Place
London W1M 9DL

Jane Churchill
118 Garrat Lane
London SW18 4DJ

Jason D'Souza Ltd
38 Graham Street
London N1 8JX

John Boyd Textiles Ltd
Higher Flax Mills
Castle Cary
Somerset BA7 7DY

John Stefanidis & Assoc Ltd
Unit 7
ChelseaWharf
Lots Road
London SW10 0QJ

Laura Ashley
27 Bagleys Lane
London SW6 2BW

Liberty of London Print
313 Merton Road
London SW18 5JS

Lelievre (UK) Ltd
16 Berners Street
London W1P 3DD

Lennox Money
93 Pimlico Road
London SW1W 8PH

Manuel Canovas Ltd
2 North Terrace
Brompton Road
London SW3 2BA

Marvic Textiles Ltd
3 Westpoint Trading Estate
Alliance Road
London W3 0RA

Mary Fox Linton
45 Hewlett House
Havelock Terrace
London SW8 4AS

Monkwell Ltd
10-12 Wharfdale Road
Bournemouth
Dorset BH4 9BT

Mulberry Company
The Rookery
Chilcompton
Bath BA3 4EH

Muriel Short Designs
Hewitts Estate
Elmbridge Road
Cranleigh
Surrey GU6 8LW

Nina Campbell
(distributed by Osborne & Little, see below)

Nobilis Fontan
1 & 2 Cedar Studio
45 Glebe Place
London SW3 5JE

Nursery Window
81 Walton Street
London SW3 2HP

Osborne & Little Plc
49 Temperley Road
London SW12 8QE

Percheron
97-99 Cleveland Street
London W1P 5PN

Pierre Frey
253 Fulham Road
London SW3 6HY

Ramm, Son & Crocker Ltd
Chiltern House
Knaves Beech Business Centre
Loudwater
High Wycombe
Buckinghamshire
HP10 9QR

Romo Ltd
Lowmoor Road
Kirkby-in-Ashfield
Nottinghamshire NG17 7DE

Sahco Hesslein UK Ltd
24 Chelsea Garden Market
Chelsea Harbour
London SW10 0XE

Sanderson
100 Acres
Oxford Road
Uxbridge
Middlesex UB8 1HY

Souleiado
171 Fulham Road
London SW3

Stuart Renaissance Textiles
Barrington Court
Barrington, Ilminster
Somerset TA19 0NQ

The Design Archives
PO Box 1464
Bournemouth
Dorset BH4 9YQ

The Malabar Cotton Co
The Coach House
Bakery Place
119 Altenburg Gardens
London SW11 1JQ

Thomas Dare
341 Kings Road
London SW3 5ES

Timney Fowler
388 Kings Road
London SW3 5UZ

Titley & Marr Ltd
141 Station Road
Liss
Hampshire GU33 7AJ

Today Interiors Ltd
Hollis Road
Grantham
Lincolnshire NG31 7QH

Turnell & Gigon
Unit M 20
Chelsea Garden Market
London SW10 0XE

Van Schelle & Gurland
1 Cambridge Road
London SW11 4RT

Warner Fabrics Plc
Bradbourne Drive
Tilbrook
Buckinghamshire MK7 8BE

Watts & Co Furnishings
7 Tufton Street
London SW1P 3QB

Wemyss/Wemyss Houlès
40 Newman Street
London W1P 3PA

Wendy Cushing Ltd
Unit M7
Chelsea Garden Market
Chelsea Harbour
London SW10 0XE

Zoffany
63 South Audley Street
London W1Y 5BF

Zimmer-Rohde
65 Chelsea Garden Market
Chelsea Harbour
London SW10 0XE

In the US:

Alan Campbell
979 Third Avenue
New York
New York 10022

Boussac of France
979 Third Avenue
New York
New York 10022

Brunschwig & Fils
979 Third Avenue
New York
New York 10022-1234

Canovas
979 Third Avenue
New York
New York 10022

Cowtan & Tout
979 Third Avenue
New York
New York 10022

Hinson
979 Third Avenue
New York
New York 10022

Jack Lenor Larsen
41 East 11th Street
New York
New York 1003-4685

Lee Jofa
979 Third Avenue
New York
New York 10022

Pierre Deux
870 Madison Avenue
New York
New York 10003

Ralph Lauren
979 Third Avenue
New York
New York 10022

Randolph & Hein
1 Arkansas Street
San Francisco
California 94107

Schumacher
International Ltd
939 Third Avenue
New York
New York 10022

Stroheim & Romann
31-11 Thomson Avenue
Long Island City
New York 11101

In France:

Braquenie
111 boulevard
Beaumarchais
75003 Paris

Burger et Cie
39 rue des Petits Champs
75001 Paris

Chanee-Ducrocq
25 rue de Clery
75002 Paris

Chotard
5 rue du Mail
75002 Paris

Edmond Petit
23 rue du Mail
75002 Paris

Etamine
2 rue de Furstemberg
75006 Paris

Deschemaker
22 rue de Mail
75002 Paris

Lauer
5 avenue de l'Opéra
75001 Paris

Lelievre
13 rue du Mail
75002 Paris

Manuel Canovas
125 rue de la Faifanderie
75116 Paris

Nobilis-Fontan
29 rue Bonaparte
75006 Paris

Pierre Frey
47 rue des Petits Champs
75001 Paris

Prelle
5 place des Victoires
75001 Paris

Souleiado
39 rue Proudhom
B.P. 21
13151 Tarascon Cedex

THE WORK OF THE FOLLOWING PROFESSIONAL INTERIOR DESIGNERS FEATURES THROUGHOUT THE BOOK, THEY MAY BE CONTACTED AT THE ADDRESSES LISTED BELOW. SEE ACKNOWLEDGMENTS, ON PAGE 192 FOR PICTURE CREDITS.

In the UK:

Roger Banks-Pye
Colefax and Fowler
119 Fulham Road
London SW3

Shireen Faircloth
42 Anselm Road
London SW6 1LJ

Anna Thomas
3 Montpellier Row
Twickenham
Middlesex TW1 2NA

Sasha Waddell
4 Delaford Street
London SW6 7LT

Karen White ISID
9 Stanley Crescent
London W11

In the US:

Ginger Barber ASID
1925 Westheimer
Houston
Texas 77098

Nancy Braithwaite
2995 Lookout Place
Atlanta
Georgia 30305

Clark/Le Cuyer Interior
Design, Robert Clark ISID
and Raymond Le Cuyer ISID
333 West 57th Street
New York
New York 110019-311

Kim DePole Design
75 East 7th Street
Suite 6B
New York
New York 10003

Michael de Santis Inc
1110 Second Avenue
New York
New York 10022

Mary Drysdale Design
Assoc Inc
1133 20th Street NW
Suite 700
Washington DC 20036

Marilyn Glass Inc
311 East 38th Street
New York
New York 10016

Carol Glasser ASID
PO Box 130246
Houston
Texas 77219-0246

Mariette Himes Gomez ASID
506/504 East 74th Street
New York
New York 100

Richard Holley ASID
1215 Oakdale
Houston
Texas 77004

Stephen and Gail Huberman
Interior Design
127 East 59th Street
New York
New York 10022

Beverly Jacomini ASID
1701 Brun Street
Houston
Texas 77019

Richard Keith Langham
18 East 67th Street
New York
New York 10021

Tonin MacCallum Inc ASID
21 East 90th Street
New York
New York 10128

Virginia Mae Witbeck
829 Park Avenue
New York
New York 10021

Charlotte Moss and
Company
16 East 65th Street
New York
New York 10021

Brett Nestler
350 East 79th Street
New York
New York 10021

Vincente Wolf Assoc Inc
333 West 39th Street
New York
New York 10018

In France:

Marie Gouny
5 rue de Charronne
75011 Paris

Stephanie Vatelot
Chateau de Reignac
33450 Saint Loubes
Bordeaux

INDEX